iPHONE 14 PRO MAX SENIORS GUIDE

Your Step-by-Step Manual to Simplify iOS,
Making It Accessible and Enjoyable for
Non-Tech-Savvy Seniors

John Halbert

TABLE OF CONTENTS

INTRODUCTION

For many seniors today, smartphones like the iPhone 14 Pro Max seem needlessly complex. With its sleek design and powerful technology packed into a compact device, this small wonder of a phone almost appears intentionally bewildering. For those who did not grow up with digital technology, terms like iOS, megapixels, and Wi-Fi can feel like a foreign language. Simply making a call or sending a text message can be frustratingly difficult.

It's no wonder that countless seniors end up relegated to only using the bare basics of their iPhones if they use them at all. This is incredibly unfortunate, as these devices offer seniors amazing opportunities to stay connected, informed, engaged, and independent. The digital world is full of resources that can meaningfully enhance seniors' lives, from video calling loved ones to accessing news or entertainment with just a tap. But without a simplified, accessible guide to using today's complex smartphones, many seniors find themselves excluded from these benefits.

As a seasoned tech enthusiast with a background in senior care, I understand the unique challenges the non-tech-savvy elderly face with modern technology. I have seen firsthand the isolation and frustration caused by devices that seem impossibly unintuitive. But I also know that with the proper guidance tailored to seniors' needs, mastering an iPhone is absolutely achievable for them. The key is presenting the information in a simplified, step-by-step manner that empowers seniors rather than overwhelming them.

My passion for simplifying complex tech concepts and enhancing the lives of seniors ultimately drove me to write this book. *iPhone 14 Pro Max Seniors Guide* aims to make using this incredible device not only manageable but highly enjoyable for older, non-technical adults. With the knowledge imparted in these pages, seniors can gain the confidence to fully utilize their iPhones and thrive in our digital era.

In this comprehensive guide, we strip away all the tech jargon and assume the reader has zero prior experience with smartphones. We start from square one, familiarizing you with the physical device, navigating the touch screen interface, managing apps, and performing basic functions like calling and texting with simplicity and clarity. Gradually, we cover more advanced features of iOS, allowing you to get the most out of your iPhone 14 Pro Max camera, apps, settings, and more.

Throughout the tutorials, the emphasis remains on simplifying processes, using plain, accessible language, and instilling confidence in even the most tech-averse senior. You will learn not through intimidation but through encouragement. My goal is that by the time you turn the final page of this guide, you feel empowered to embrace this technology on your own terms.

Using an iPhone - or any smartphone - should never be an exercise in frustration but rather an opportunity to enrich your life. By learning iOS in a gradual, stress-free manner, you can unlock doors to independence, social engagement, entertainment, and knowledge right in your pocket. You will discover just how effortless and enjoyable using an iPhone can be when presented the right way.

If you have ever felt overwhelmed, defeated, or skeptical of mastering new technology in your golden years, prepare to have your outlook changed. This book will equip you with the exact knowledge and techniques you need to navigate your iPhone 14 Pro Max like a pro. So read on, absorb each lesson, and start getting the most from your device today!

CHAPTER 1

IPHONE 14 PRO MAX BASICS

| Understanding the Device

Apple's newest iPhone model, the iPhone 14 Pro Max, represents the pinnacle of the company's smartphone technology and design. As the successor to last year's iPhone 13 Pro Max, the iPhone 14 Pro Max delivers noteworthy upgrades while retaining the premium build quality and performance that users expect from Apple's Pro lineup.

With a starting price of $1099, the iPhone 14 Pro Max is clearly positioned as a luxury smartphone aimed at tech enthusiasts, creative professionals, and status-conscious consumers. At that lofty price point, prospective buyers will rightfully have high expectations for what the phone can deliver. This article will provide an in-depth look at the iPhone 14 Pro Max, from its hardware capabilities and new features to real-world performance and hands-on impressions, to help readers understand precisely what they'll be getting for the money.

Hardware & Design

At first glance, the iPhone 14 Pro Max looks strikingly similar to last year's model, with the same flat-edged stainless steel design and "notch" cutout at the top of the display. Look closer, however, and some subtle but meaningful changes become apparent. The notch is now smaller, the rear camera bump protrudes less, and the whole chassis has a more refined look and feel.

With a 6.7-inch OLED display, the Pro Max retains the same expansive screen size as its predecessor. Image quality is excellent, with vivid colors, inky blacks, and outstanding brightness topping out at up to 2000 nits for HDR content. The display now features Apple's new "Dynamic Island," which eliminates the notch by using software to make the remaining front-facing hardware blend into the background.

On the inside, Apple has outfitted the iPhone 14 Pro Max with its latest A16 Bionic chip. Fabricated on a cutting-edge 4nm process node, the A16 has nearly 16 billion transistors and 6 high-performance CPU cores. Combined with a 5-core GPU and enhanced neural engine, the A16 delivers breezy performance across the board. Real-world speed is effortlessly fast, even in demanding games and apps.

The iPhone 14 Pro Max matches that power with a generous 6GB of RAM and storage options of up to 1 TB. Battery life is excellent as well, thanks to the phone's 4323 mAh battery. Apple claims the 14 Pro Max lasts up to 29 hours on video playback, which matches up with real-world experience. The phone has no issues lasting a full day of heavy use.

Cameras are a major focus, with the iPhone 14 Pro Max bringing Apple's latest photography tech. The main wide camera uses a 48MP sensor for the first time, enabling pixel binning for 12MP shots with enhanced low-light capture. The ultra-wide camera matches the 13 Pro Max, while the telephoto gets a boost to 3x optical zoom. The TrueDepth selfie camera sees the resolution bumped to 12MP.

Dynamic Island & Always-On Display

Among the headline new features for the iPhone 14 Pro models are the Dynamic Island and Always-On display. These build on the design and display changes mentioned earlier to provide new ways for users to interact with the phone.

The Dynamic Island is one of the most visually striking changes on the new iPhones. Located at the top center of the display, it replaces the notch by blending the remaining front hardware into the background using software tricks. Icons and alerts animate up from Dynamic Island, acting as an at-a-glance notification center. Tap and hold allows access to music controls, timers, and other quick settings.

Complementing the Dynamic Island is the new Always-On display capability. As the name suggests, the display remains persistently illuminated at a dimmed setting to show the clock, widgets, and live wallpaper, even when the phone is locked. This allows users to quickly check info like the time and notifications without needing to wake or unlock the phone.

The Always-On display is enabled through a 1Hz refresh rate when inactive. Once unlocked, the display leaps back to full brightness at up to 120Hz for silky smooth scrolling and animations. Cleverly, the Always-On display disables itself temporarily when certain conditions are met to save battery life, like when the phone is face down or in a pocket.

For Android users, neither the Dynamic Island nor Always-On display will seem revolutionary, as similar features have been available for years. But both represent major steps forward for iOS and provide visual differentiation between iPhone 14 Pro models and the standard 14. Their addition brings tangible new ways to interact with the iPhone that build on Apple's strengths in hardware and software integration.

Performance & Battery Life

As mentioned earlier, the iPhone 14 Pro Max is powered by Apple's latest A16 Bionic chip, which offers substantial performance gains over last year's A15. The 6-core CPU and 5-core GPU, paired with the enhanced 16-core Neural Engine, provide swift and responsive performance across the iOS interface in demanding games, editing 8K video, and more.

In benchmarks, the A16 posts single-core CPU scores over 1700 on Geekbench 5, showing solid gains versus the iPhone 13 Pro Max. Graphics and machine learning tasks show similar leaps versus the already extremely powerful A15. For a mobile chip to keep delivering double-digit percentage improvements year-over-year is seriously impressive.

Of course, synthetic benchmarks can only reveal so much about real-world experience. In daily use, the iPhone 14 Pro Max flaunts its power through buttery smooth navigation, apps that pop open instantly, and demanding workloads that are handled with ease. Even in mobile games with console-level graphics, the 14 Pro Max doesn't break a sweat.

Apple has optimized iOS 16 to take advantage of the A16's muscle with slick new features like the customizable lock screen. Third-party apps also benefit, though many current titles were developed with older iPhones in mind. The true capabilities of the A16 may not be fully tapped for another year or two as developers update their software.

Battery life is another strength, with Apple making sensible optimizations like scaling the refresh rate down to 1Hz on the Always-On display. In practice, the iPhone 14 Pro Max easily delivers an all-day battery even with heavy use. Screen time of 8 hours plus is achievable, especially if you skip power-hungry tasks like gaming. Overall battery benchmarks show a modest bump versus the 13 Pro Max of around 12%, resulting in the excellent real-world performance mentioned earlier. 30 minutes of charging adds up to 50% battery, while a full charge takes about 90 minutes. Wireless MagSafe charging is supported up to 15W.

For those who need their phone to keep going morning to night, the iPhone 14 Pro Max won't disappoint. The combination of a powerhouse A16 chip plus all-day battery life means you never need to worry about the phone slowing down or needing a top-up before the day's end. It's ready to work as hard as you do.

Camera Upgrades

The iPhone camera system has been a staple of Apple's success over the years, always keeping pace with or exceeding the competition. With the iPhone 14 Pro Max, Apple brings its sharpest set of upgrades yet, headlined by a jump to 48 megapixels for the main wide camera. This ushers in a new era for iPhone photography.

That 48MP quad-pixel sensor captures so much resolution that Apple is implementing pixel binning to combine data from groups of 4 pixels into one large 12MP pixel. The result is much improved low-light performance, as evidenced by night mode shots that reveal crisp details even in near darkness. The larger pixels also enable a 2x zoom mode dubbed "Optical Zoom Out" that provides a wider field of view ideal for landscapes.

Standard 12MP shots in the daytime exhibit the typically excellent exposure and color you'd expect from iPhone cameras. Detail and sharpness have taken a noticeable step up versus the 13 Pro Max thanks to the higher resolution sensor. The improvements Apple has eked out of its image processing chips over the years are constantly impressive.

The other big camera upgrade comes on the telephoto end, where optical zoom now reaches 3x versus 2x on last year's model. This provides a 77mm equivalent focal length that is perfect for portraits and other mid-range zoom needs. Apple smartly chose 3x rather than a longer zoom range to optimize for quality rather than max specs. Combined with the main camera's 2x zoom out, the 14 Pro Max covers an ideal range of focal lengths.

The ultra-wide camera delivers a 120-degree field of view, great for landscapes and tight spaces. This year's ƒ/2.2 aperture improves light capture over earlier models. Photographic styles like rich contrast and vibrant warm filters can be applied to all three cameras. Video support extends up to 4K 60fps with Dolby Vision HDR across all rear cameras and the TrueDepth selfie camera.

Setting Up Your iPhone

You've just taken your shiny new iPhone 14 Pro Max out of the box. As impressive as it looks and feels, some work is required to get your phone programmed for your preferences and ready to use. This process is known as initial setup, and it lays the foundation for everything that follows. Done right, the initial setup makes your iPhone uniquely yours, tailored to your needs and how you work. Here's an in-depth look at the setup process and key choices new users face when firing up an iPhone 14 Pro Max for the first time.

The First Boot Experience

Power on your new iPhone 14 Pro Max, and you'll be greeted with the time-honored "Hello" in a multitude of languages. This is where the initial setup experience begins. You'll be walked through the process by a series of prompts to connect to Wi-Fi, login with or create an Apple ID, enable key features, and configure basic settings. Apple has refined this process over the years to make it quick and straightforward, but there are still choices to consider.

If available, connecting to a Wi-Fi network during setup ensures you can enable key features like iCloud backup and Apple ID login. Make sure the network requires no additional login or verification beyond the password. If no trusted network is available, you can skip this step and continue setting up the iPhone using cellular data. A Wi-Fi connection will still be prompted later in the setup.

Next comes the all-important Apple ID creation or login. Your Apple ID acts as the master key that unlocks access to Apple services and stores your personal data. If you're new to Apple devices, take a moment to create a memorable Apple ID using an email you control. If you have an existing Apple ID tied to other devices, simply enter your credentials to log in. Using your existing ID enables seamless syncing of data across your ecosystem.

With your Apple ID authenticated, you'll have the option to restore the iPhone from an iCloud or iTunes backup containing your apps, data, and settings. For brand new users, starting fresh is recommended to fully experience the onboarding process. But for existing Apple users, loading a backup instantly configures the device with your preferences. Apps can always be downloaded again later if needed.

Essential Options and Features

With the formalities out of the way, the initial setup shifts focus to enabling key features and options. Here, you have an opportunity to personalize your preferences. Location services can be set to on or off system-wide. Analytics and improvement data can be shared with or withheld from Apple. Display zoom offers larger interface elements for those with visual needs. And you'll select your default language and region settings.

Next up are security choices like setting up Face ID by scanning your face from multiple angles. Face ID replacement for passwords is quick and convenient, so it's worth taking a moment to set up properly. Passcode creation, meanwhile, adds an extra layer of protection. Skip both for convenience at the cost of security. A passcode is required for some features, however, like parental restrictions.

With basic preferences established, you'll advance to service activation. Here, Apple presents toggles for enabling iCloud sync, Find My location tracking, sharing analytics, Siri, dictation, App Store downloads, and more. For most users, the defaults are recommended, but power users may wish to tweak these settings further post-setup.

Finally, you'll confirm Apple's storage, usage, and privacy policies and be offered the option to enable Wallet for Apple Pay. Biometric sign-in for banking and finance apps is also presented. And with that, you arrive at the iPhone home screen, ready to start personalizing your apps and data.

Optimizing Settings to Your Needs

The initial setup flow gives you the bare essential options for activation. But, a much deeper configuration is possible within the Settings app to further tailor the iPhone experience. Here are some additional settings new users may wish to examine and configure:

- Display & Brightness: Enable Auto-Brightness and True Tone if desired. Set refresh rate to Standard or High as preferred.
- Wallpaper: Change default wallpapers to personal images.
- Notification settings: Tweak delivered-quietly schedules, app notifications, and Lock Screen appearance.
- Control Center: Add/remove controls like Dark Mode, screen recording, and accessibility shortcuts.
- General keyboard settings: Configure autocorrection, prediction, spell check, and shortcuts.

- Camera: Enable/disable formats like HEIF, Macro Control, and Auto HDR based on preference.
- Siri & Search: Disable/enable suggest and announce notifications, show Siri on the lock screen, and listen for "Hey Siri."
- Safari: Toggle privacy protections, security, content blocking, default search engine, and other preferences.
- Messages: Activate handoff on additional devices, disable Share Name/Photo, etc.
- Wallet & Apple Pay: Add credit/debit cards, enable Express Transit cards, adjust default card, shipping address, etc.
- App Store: Toggle automatic downloads, cellular download limits, and optional apps.

Take time to thoroughly explore the Settings app and custom-tailor your preferences. Your iPhone will become more uniquely yours and optimized for how you work as you configure options to your needs.

Loading Up Your Apps

With setup complete, it's time to populate your iPhone 14 Pro Max with all your favorite apps and games. For new users, exploring the App Store is a great way to discover amazing iOS apps across categories like social, messaging, entertainment, productivity, finance, and more. Downloading apps directly from the App Store ensures you're getting fully-optimized official versions.

Existing Apple users will want to install apps purchased previously using their Apple ID. The easiest route is to restore an iCloud backup, which automatically re-downloads your purchased apps. Alternatively, you can manually search and install previously purchased apps by tapping your profile icon in the App Store. This route lets you cherry-pick which apps get installed rather than restoring everything.

Keep in mind the iPhone 14 Pro Max boasts an enormous screen ideal for Apple Arcade gaming. Be sure to browse gaming categories and try out visually stunning titles like Oceanhorn 2, FANTASIAN and the NBA 2K series. Apple Arcade offers loads of exclusive games free for subscribers.

And don't neglect built-in apps like Safari, Apple Maps, News, Stocks, Health, and more. Set default apps under Settings to override Apple's own with third-party options if desired. With all your apps loaded up and your home screen arranged your iPhone is ready to slot into your life.

CHAPTER 2

NAVIGATING IOS SIMPLIFIED

Exploring The User Interface

For new iPhone users, the clean simplicity of the iOS interface can seem both appealing and intimidating. Devoid of the clutter and complex menus of other platforms, the iPhone UI relies on gestures and spatial memory to get around. But behind that minimalist exterior lies deep functionality waiting to be unlocked. This guide will walk you through the key aspects of the iOS interface on the iPhone 14 Pro and offer tips to master navigation.

The Home Screen

The home screen is command central on your iPhone, providing quick access to key apps and system functions. Arranged in a familiar grid, apps can be placed wherever desired or automatically sorted. The dock along the bottom enables one-tap access to your most used apps. Swipe right to access widgets like weather, news, and calendar events. Swipe left to access search and proactive Siri App Suggestions.

Press and hold on app icons to enter "jiggle mode" for management options. Double-press the home button to access Apple Pay and other shortcuts. It all starts here.

Swipe down from the top bezel to reveal the Notification Center and view alerts conveniently grouped by app. Time, battery %, and wireless connections are shown at a glance. You can clear notifications or tap to expand them for more info and actions. Swipe right across an alert to access notification settings for that app.

Swipe up from the bottom bezel or press the home button to return to the home screen from within apps. This replaces the Back button in other mobile operating systems. Over time, your muscle memory will develop to instinctively swipe up to exit apps.

Mastering Multitasking

Multitasking on the iPhone allows running multiple apps at once and quickly switching between them. To view open apps, swipe up from the bottom and pause halfway. The App Switcher shows preview cards of open apps that you can shuffle through horizontally. Flick apps up to close them or tap to return. Hold an app preview for quick actions like opening a split view.

Frequently used app combinations can be paired in Split View via the App Switcher. This displays both apps simultaneously side-by-side. Split View is ideal for copying info between apps or viewing two apps at once, like email and messages.

Slide Over lets you overlay an app on top of another in a floating window. Swipe right from the right edge of the screen to access your most recently used app in Slide Over. Quickly swap apps from the App Switcher while retaining your main app underneath.

Picture in Picture shrinks a video down to a movable floating window, perfect for watching video while multitasking. Tap the PiP control to return the video to full screen.

With practice, these gestures become second nature. App switching enables workflows not possible on mobile before.

Navigating Apps

Within apps themselves, interface conventions will start feeling familiar with use. Tap buttons, icons, and options to activate features. Tap the back buttons in the upper left to return to the previous screens.

Many apps employ a tab bar at the bottom for quick navigation between sections. The Camera app uses a modal interface to switch modes like Photo, Video, and Portrait.

Swipe right or use the back buttons to go back. Pinch and spread to zoom in on maps and images. Shake the phone gently to undo typing. These and other gestures streamline navigation.

Finding Hidden Features

Digging deeper reveals advanced features that are not obvious at a glance. Press and hold buttons and icons to uncover additional options via pop-up menus. Touch and hold the keyboard space bar to access the cursor for precise text editing.

Swipe down within apps to quickly access search bars or refresh screens. Drag lists vertically to leap through alphabetical sections for rapid scrolling.

Try Force Touch or hard press on elements to surface useful quick actions. Learn optimal use patterns for apps like Mail, Safari, Photos, Notes and more to operate more efficiently.

Apple has meticulously designed iOS as a tactile, gesture-based interface. Learning the hidden features accelerates productivity.

Customizing the Experience

While iOS offers a consistent experience out of the box, you can tweak and customize aspects to suit personal preferences. Rearrange home screen apps by holding and dragging. Create additional home pages and populate widgets, shortcuts or folders.

Change wallpaper, font sizes, icon sizes, and themes under Settings > Display & Brightness. Switch up app icons and Home Screen options through the same menu.

Notifications can be managed app-by-app or as a whole. Deliver Quietly, deliver on Lock Screen, sounds, and badges are all configurable per app.

Create custom vibration patterns, default apps, Siri shortcuts, and more under Settings to tailor how you interact with iOS. Add accessibility features to assist vision, mobility, hearing, and cognition. The flexibility is there for the taking.

Mastering the iPhone 14 Pro

Learning to intuitively navigate iOS does take time and practice. But Apple has refined this interface over 15 years while preserving signature simplicity. Follow these tips and guides to quickly gain mastery:

- Use every app actively to acclimate to conventions and gestures. Don't be afraid to poke around.
- Add commonly used widgets, folders and shortcuts to your Home Screen for quick access.
- Swipe often from screen edges to reveal hidden menus and access multitasking.
- Play with Focus modes, wallpapers, vibration patterns and ringtone creation.
- Fully explore Settings for deep customization and accessibility options.
- Review Apple's guided tips or schedule a session with Apple Support for hands-on help.

The iPhone 14 Pro offers a premium hardware experience. Pair that with mastering the iOS interface through helpful resources like this, and you have a powerful device tailored precisely to you. User experience defines Apple. Learn to use that experience to empower your life and productivity on iPhone 14 Pro.

| Mastering Touch Gestures

The expansive 6.7-inch display of the iPhone 14 Pro Max is a canvas for performing some of the most intuitive and powerful gestures available on a smartphone. iOS provides a tactile, intuitive interface built around common gestures like tap, swipe, drag, pinch, and press. Mastering these touch gestures is the key to operating your iPhone 14 Pro Max efficiently. This guide will break down the essential gestures and offer tips to incorporate them into your workflows.

Tap

The tap is the most basic iOS gesture, used for activating buttons, selecting items, and entering text via the on-screen keyboard. Tapping icons on the home screen launches apps while tapping Back buttons exits screens. Double tap to zoom into images and webpages or to trigger Apple Pay. The tap offers precision interaction, perfect for compact touch targets.

Get in the habit of accurately targeting interface elements with fingertip taps. Avoid using nails or tapping too forcefully. For smaller links and buttons, zooming in helps land accurate taps. Keyboard typing develops rhythmic tap skills. As the fundamental gesture, master taps for effortless iOS control.

Swipe

Swiping involves quickly dragging your finger across the iPhone's display to activate certain functions. Swipe down from the top bezel to reveal the Notification Center. Swipe up from the bottom bezel to go home or enter the App Switcher. Swipe left and right to switch between home screen pages.

Swiping left on notifications clears them, while swiping right reveals additional options. Swipe through apps horizontally to shuffle between them in the App Switcher. Drag the keyboard space bar to move the cursor. Swiping enables efficient one-handed use, which is critical for the Pro Max's large display.

Practice horizontal, vertical, and diagonal swipes across apps to internalize this essential gesture. Swipe speed and length will trigger different actions once memorized. Smooth swiping abilities aid navigation and productivity.

Drag

Dragging allows moving interface elements by pressing, holding, and dragging your finger. You can rearrange apps on the home screen this way by dragging icons around. Dragging also enables precise text selection by holding passages and then dragging selection handles.

Use dragging to peruse long documents and webpages by simply scrolling through content. Drag notifications and widgets downwards for quick management options. Drag horizontally to skip through pages and tabs.

Dragging promotes spatial awareness in iOS through direct manipulation. Practice selecting, moving, and acting on screen elements via smooth dragging motions.

Pinch and Spread

iOS employs multi-touch gestures like pinch and spread for resizing and zooming. Pinch two fingers together to shrink maps, webpages, and photos. Spread fingers apart to enlarge the same. These gestures provide nuanced control over iOS content.

Utilize pinching and spreading for legible reading of text, detailed map navigation, and inspecting images closely. Learn optimal pinch and spread finger placement and motion. On the Pro Max's expansive display, sizing content precisely is a must.

Stretch and compress fingers in a natural pinching/spreading motion. Allow the side of the finger to glide on the glass rather than just the tips for fluid interaction. Practice resizing until pinch and spread feel effortless.

Press and Hold

Pressing and holding on elements reveals additional options and information via pop-up menus. Press and hold app icons to enter "jiggle mode" for management. Hold links and images for quick interaction choices. Try pressing and holding buttons and icons for hidden functionality.

On the keyboard, press and hold modifiers like Command, Option, and Shift to access special characters and punctuation. Hold the space bar to maneuver the cursor. Press and hold offers a right-click style utility on iOS.

Take time to deeply press screen elements to uncover useful menus. But avoid forcefully mashing the display. The iPhone's pressure-sensitive 3D Touch has been replaced by the Haptic Touch, requiring only a normal press.

Advanced Gestures

Once you've mastered the above essentials, exploring more advanced gestures opens up additional skills:

- Swipe left/right across the bottom edge to switch between apps.
- Swipe diagonally to return to the previous app.
- Double tap (don't fully press) the side button for Apple Pay.
- Hard press display while dragging to enter selection mode.
- Swipe left or right with two fingers to switch Safari tabs.
- Spread three fingers to cut/copy/paste/undo.
- Pinch four fingers together to close an app.

Take time to absorb the nuances of multi-finger and edge/bezel gestures to command your iPhone like a pro. Customize the Accessibility setting for your needs. On the spacious Pro Max display, hand gymnastics become worthwhile.

Mastering Natural Motion

Approaching iOS gestures with care and precision promotes fluid interaction. Use relaxed, natural finger motions rather than rigid jabs and pokes. Let fingers glide across the smooth display glass to execute effective gestures. iOS was designed with the human hand and body in mind.

Ergonomic techniques like resting palms while tapping or pinching avoid discomfort or fatigue. Adjust hand positioning often rather than remaining static in one stressful pose. Leverage comfortable swiping and dragging across the full screen.

The expansive canvas of the iPhone 14 Pro Max gives you room to get creative. Two-handed gestures utilizing both thumbs streamline operation. The Pro Max screen real estate reduces cramping or clustered finger placement.

Bridging the Physical and Digital

Mastering touch gestures forms the crucial physical connection between the user and the interface. Skilled gesture use mesh the digital environment of iOS with familiar human movement. Your iPhone becomes an intuitive extension of your body rather than just a tool.

So take time practicing the key taps, swipes, pinches, and presses that form your touch vocabulary. Utilize Accessibility settings as needed. Soon gestures will flow naturally as your hands learn the iPhone dance. Pushing beyond the basics reveals advanced gestures that unlock next-level productivity. Let the tips here guide your journey toward touch proficiency on the iPhone 14 Pro Max.

Managing Apps and Notifications

As magnificent and powerful as the iPhone 14 Pro Max may be, like any device, it has the potential to become overwhelmed without proper organization and maintenance. With a library of apps and notifications constantly vying for attention, keeping things streamlined takes some deliberate effort. But with a few simple steps, 14 Pro Max owners can curate calm and stay focused on what truly matters.

The first task is to purge unnecessary apps from the home screens. When was the last time certain apps were actually opened? Uninstalling rarely used titles declutters and optimizes storage. As part of spring cleaning, go through the home pages one by one, thoughtfully rearranging core apps for seamless access as well.

Once home screens are only housing must-haves, it's time to utilize the hidden App Library. Access it by swiping past the last home page to enter a folder-like view alphabetically listing every installed app. Less core titles can live here out of sight until needed. Now the home screens serve a clear purpose without anything extra weighing them down.

From the Home Screen, open the Settings app and select "Notifications" from the menu. Here, granular controls appear for customizing alerts sent from each app individually. Disable unnecessary sounds and pop-ups, like muting email alerts or allowing only silent social media notifications. Prioritizing critical updates maintains focus.

For communicative apps, ensure only notifications from VIPs like close friends and family interrupt peaceful flows. Otherwise, downgrade alerts to subtle badges visible on the always-on display. This option is perfect for apps where staying generally informed is valuable without jarring interruptions.

Going further, the new "Unknown App Alerts" setting blocks mystery prompts entirely until an unrecognized notification source is verified as safe, circumventing strange distractions. And "Manage Notification Groups" refines how contact alerts are merged for clean overall messages.

Now that settings are tailored, some 14 Pro Max tricks simplify dismissing existing notifications. Control Center accessed with a swipe lets users instantly mute problematic apps or delete all notifications with ease. And Focus modes can autoblock selected interrupters during important windows.

Regular maintenance prevents issues down the line too. Periodically review installed apps to remove unused titles, always-on settings to ensure relevance, and notification privileges to confirm appropriateness. Tweaks over time adapt the system to evolving needs and priorities, like adjusting parameters when responsibilities change.

Through these simple organization habits, the powerful iPhone 14 Pro Max remains joyous to operate - increased control over apps and alerts grants mental clarity. Thoughtful curation transforms it from a source of potential distraction to a transparent tool serving focused priorities and relationships above all else. Welcome tranquility is the reward for residents making these significant but minimal efforts.

CHAPTER 3

COMMUNICATION AND CONNECTION

In today's fast-paced digital age, staying connected with loved ones and friends has become an essential part of our daily lives. The iPhone 14 Pro Max, with its impressive array of features and user-friendly interface, is a fantastic tool for seniors to enhance their communication and connection experiences. In Chapter 3 of our guide, we will take you through a comprehensive journey of mastering communication and connection on your iPhone 14 Pro Max.

We will break down the chapter into three main sections: making calls and sending messages, using FaceTime and video calls, and managing email, contacts, and social media. By the end of this guide, you'll feel confident in your ability to navigate the world of digital communication using your iPhone 14 Pro Max.

| Making Calls and Sending Messages

Making Calls

One of the primary functions of any mobile phone is making calls, and your iPhone 14 Pro Max is no exception. Here's a step-by-step guide on how to make calls with your device:

1. Unlock Your iPhone Begin by unlocking your iPhone. You can do this by pressing the side button (located on the right-hand side of the device) or using Face ID if you have it set up.
2. Access the Phone App Locate the green Phone app icon on your home screen, which features a white phone receiver icon inside a green square. Tap on it to open the app.
3. Dial a Number In the Phone app, you'll see a numeric keypad. To dial a number, tap the digits on the keypad. If you're calling someone from your contacts, you can start typing their name or number, and your iPhone will suggest matches as you type.
4. Place the Call Once you've entered the number or selected a contact, tap the green call button (depicted by a white phone receiver icon). This will initiate the call.
5. End the Call To end the call, simply tap the red "End Call" button that appears on the screen during the call.

Sending Messages

Sending text messages, also known as SMS (Short Message Service) or iMessages, is another crucial aspect of communication. Here's how you can send messages on your iPhone 14 Pro Max:

1. Unlock Your iPhone Just like with making calls, start by unlocking your iPhone.
2. Access the Messages App Locate the Messages app icon on your home screen. It has a green speech bubble icon. Tap on it to open the app.
3. Compose a New Message To compose a new message, tap the pencil icon (usually found in the upper-right or upper-left corner of the screen, depending on your iOS version). This will open a new message window.
4. Select Recipient In the "To:" field, enter the name or phone number of the person you want to send the message to. As you type, your iPhone will suggest contacts from your address book.
5. Compose Your Message Once you've selected the recipient, tap the text field at the bottom of the screen and start typing your message. You can also add emojis, photos, or other attachments by tapping the icons located to the left of the text field.
6. Send the Message When your message is ready, tap the blue send button (depicted by an upward-pointing arrow) to send it. Your message will be delivered to the recipient.

Managing Calls and Messages

It's essential to know how to manage your calls and messages effectively. Here are some additional tips:

Call Logs

To view your call history, open the Phone app and tap the "Recents" tab. Here, you can see a list of recent calls, including missed calls, received calls, and dialed calls.

Message Threads

In the Messages app, your conversations are organized into threads. Tap on a thread to view the entire conversation with that contact.

Notifications

Your iPhone will notify you of missed calls and new messages. You can customize notification settings in the Settings app under "Notifications."

Do Not Disturb

If you want to silence calls and notifications temporarily, you can enable the "Do Not Disturb" mode in the Control Center or Settings.

Blocking Contacts

To block unwanted calls and messages, you can add numbers to your blocked contacts list. Find this option in the Settings app under "Phone" and "Messages."

| Using FaceTime and Video Calls

Introduction to FaceTime

FaceTime is Apple's video and audio calling service that allows you to have face-to-face conversations with friends and family, even if they are miles away. Here's how to use FaceTime on your iPhone 14 Pro Max:

- Access FaceTime Tap the FaceTime app icon on your home screen. It features a white video camera icon inside a green square.
- Sign in with Your Apple ID If you're not already signed in, you'll need to sign in with your Apple ID. If you don't have one, you can create an Apple ID in the Settings app.
- Start a FaceTime Call To start a FaceTime call, tap the plus (+) button in the top-right corner. Enter the name, phone number, or email address of the person you want to call and tap their contact card.
- Make the Call Tap either the video camera icon to initiate a video call or the phone icon for an audio call. Your call will connect, and you'll see and hear the other person on your screen.

FaceTime Features

FaceTime offers various features to enhance your video and audio calling experience:

- Switch Cameras: During a FaceTime call, you can switch between the front and rear cameras by tapping the camera icon with arrows.
- Mute and End Call: You can mute your microphone by tapping the microphone icon, and you can end the call by tapping the red "End Call" button.
- FaceTime Effects: Spice up your calls by using FaceTime effects like Animoji, Memoji, and filters. Tap the star icon to access these features during a call.

- Group FaceTime: You can have group video calls with up to 32 participants. To start a group call, follow the same steps as for one-on-one calls and add multiple contacts.
- Screen Share: If you want to share your screen with the other person, tap the screen share icon (a rectangle with an arrow) during the call.

Tips for a Great FaceTime Experience

To ensure a smooth FaceTime experience, consider the following tips:

- A strong Wi-Fi connection will provide the best call quality. If Wi-Fi is unavailable, FaceTime can also work over cellular data, but be mindful of data usage.
- Make sure your camera is at eye level and that you are well-lit to enhance your appearance during calls.
- For better audio quality and to reduce background noise, consider using headphones with a built-in microphone.
- Video calls may consume storage space, so periodically check and free up space on your iPhone.

▎Email, Contacts, and Social Media

Managing Email

Email is a fundamental tool for communication, and your iPhone 14 Pro Max provides a seamless email experience. Here's a step-by-step guide on managing email:

1. Access the Mail App Locate the Mail app icon on your home screen. It has a white envelope icon. Tap on it to open the app.
2. Add Your Email Accounts If you haven't added your email accounts yet, tap "Add Account" and follow the on-screen instructions to add your email accounts (e.g., Gmail, Yahoo, Outlook).
3. Compose and Send Emails To compose a new email, tap the pencil icon (usually found in the bottom-right corner). Fill in the recipient's email address, subject, and message, then tap "Send."
4. Check Your Inbox Tap the "Inbox" tab to view your incoming emails. You can tap on an email to read it and respond if needed.
5. Manage Email Folders You can organize your emails by creating folders. To do this, tap "Edit" in the top-right corner, then tap "New Mailbox" to create a new folder.

Managing Contacts

Your iPhone 14 Pro Max allows you to store and manage your contacts efficiently. Here's how to do it:

1. Access the Contacts App Locate the Contacts app icon on your home screen. It features a silhouette of a person. Tap on it to open the app.
2. Add a New Contact To add a new contact, tap the plus (+) button in the top-right corner. Fill in the contact's details, such as name, phone number, and email address.

3. Edit and Delete Contacts To edit a contact's details, tap on the contact and then tap "Edit." To delete a contact, tap "Edit" and then scroll down and tap "Delete Contact."
4. Import Contacts You can import contacts from other sources like your email accounts. Tap "Settings," then "Contacts," and choose "Import SIM Contacts" or "Import from [email provider]."

Using Social Media

Social media platforms are a great way to stay connected with friends and family. Here's a general guide to using social media on your iPhone 14 Pro Max:

1. Download Social Media Apps Visit the App Store, search for the social media apps you want (e.g., Facebook, Twitter, Instagram), and download them to your iPhone.
2. Sign In or Create Accounts Once the apps are downloaded, open them and either sign in with your existing account or create new accounts if needed.
3. Explore and Connect Each social media app will have its own interface, but generally, you can explore posts, connect with friends, follow people, and share your own updates.

| CHAPTER 4 |

ENTERTAINMENT AND INFORMATION

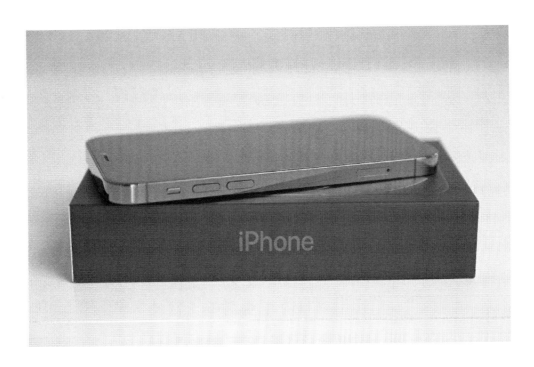

In today's fast-paced digital age, our smartphones have become more than just communication devices; they are our primary source of entertainment and information. The iPhone 14 Pro Max, with its cutting-edge features and powerful capabilities, is a device that excels in providing a seamless entertainment and information experience. In this chapter, we will delve into Chapter 4, focusing on enjoying music, videos, and podcasts, accessing news and information, and exploring the App Store for apps and games. We will provide step-by-step instructions and tips to help you make the most of your iPhone 14 Pro Max for all your entertainment and information needs.

Enjoying Music, Videos, and Podcasts

The iPhone 14 Pro Max offers a rich multimedia experience, allowing you to enjoy music, videos, and podcasts on the go. Let's explore how to get the most out of these features.

Step 1: Playing Music

1. To access your music collection, tap the "Music" app icon on your home screen.
2. In the "Library" tab, you can browse your music by playlists, artists, albums, and songs. Tap on your desired category to start listening.
3. Tap on a song title to start playing it. You can control playback by tapping the play/pause button, skipping tracks, or adjusting the volume.
4. To create a custom playlist, tap "Library" and select "Playlists." Then, tap the "+" button to create a new playlist, and add songs to it by tapping "Add Songs."

Step 2: Watching Videos

1. The "TV" app is where you can access your video content. Tap its icon on the home screen.
2. Explore movies, TV shows, and videos available for purchase, rent, or from your library. Tap on a title to view details.
3. Once you've selected a video, tap "Play" to start watching. You can control playback by pausing, rewinding, or adjusting volume.
4. Use AirPlay to stream content to a compatible TV or device for a larger viewing experience.

Step 3: Exploring Podcasts

1. Find the "Podcasts" app on your home screen and tap to open it.
2. Explore a wide range of podcasts by genre, popularity, or search for specific topics.
3. To keep up with your favorite shows, tap the "Subscribe" button. New episodes will be automatically downloaded when available.
4. Select a podcast episode to start listening. You can adjust playback speed and skip forward or backward as needed.

Accessing News and Information

Staying informed has never been easier with the iPhone 14 Pro Max. Here's how you can access news and information effortlessly.

Step 1: Apple News

1. Locate the "News" app on your home screen and tap it.
2. Browse through a wide range of news topics and sources. Tap on a topic to see related articles.
3. Tap "Following" to select your preferred news sources and customize your news feed.
4. To save an interesting article, tap the share button (the square with an arrow) and select "Add to Reading List" or "Save PDF to Books."

Step 2: Safari Browser

1. Tap the Safari icon on your home screen to launch the web browser.
2. Use the search bar at the top to enter keywords or website URLs to find information on the web.
3. Save your favorite websites by tapping the bookmark icon, and manage multiple open tabs for easy multitasking.
4. When reading articles, tap the reader icon in the address bar for a clutter-free reading experience.

Step 3: Voice Assistant - Siri

1. To access information hands-free, you can activate Siri by saying "Hey Siri" or holding down the side button.
2. You can ask Siri various questions like "What's the weather today?" or "Tell me the latest news."
3. Need directions to a place? Simply ask Siri to provide you with directions and navigation.

| Exploring the App Store for Apps and Games

The App Store is a treasure trove of apps and games that can enhance your iPhone experience. Let's dive into how you can explore and download these apps.

Step 1: Open the App Store

1. Locate the App Store icon on your home screen and tap it to open the store.
2. The front page displays featured apps and games. Swipe up and down to explore the selections.
3. Tap the search icon (a magnifying glass) and enter the name of the app or a keyword to find what you're looking for.
4. Swipe left to access different app categories like "Games," "Productivity," "Health & Fitness," and more.

Step 2: Downloading Apps

1. Once you've found an app you want to download, tap on it to view its details.
2. If the app is free, tap "Get" to download it. If it's a paid app, tap the price, and then use Face ID or Touch ID to confirm the purchase.
3. Enter your Apple ID password if prompted.
4. The app will start downloading to your home screen. You can monitor the progress by checking the app icon on your home screen.

Step 3: Managing Apps and Updates

1. To organize your apps, press and hold any app icon until they start wiggling. You can then move, delete, or create folders to better organize your apps.

2. Updates for your installed apps can be found in the "Updates" tab of the App Store. Tap "Update" next to each app to keep them current.
3. You can enable automatic app updates in your iPhone settings under "App Store." This ensures your apps are always up to date.

The iPhone 14 Pro Max is a versatile device that offers a world of entertainment and information at your fingertips. From enjoying music, videos, and podcasts to staying informed through news apps and Siri, and even exploring the vast App Store, this chapter has provided you with a comprehensive guide to making the most of your iPhone's capabilities.

As you continue to explore and use your iPhone 14 Pro Max, don't hesitate to experiment with different features and apps to tailor your device to your preferences. The iPhone is designed to adapt to your needs, and with the knowledge you've gained from this guide, you're well on your way to becoming a proficient user of this remarkable device.

| CHAPTER 5 |

PHOTOGRAPHY AND VIDEO

In today's digital age, capturing memories through photography and videography has become a fundamental part of our lives. The iPhone 14 Pro Max, with its advanced features and capabilities, offers a remarkable platform for taking high-quality photos, recording videos, and organizing your media library efficiently. In this chapter, we'll delve into the intricate details of how to maximize the potential of your iPhone 14 Pro Max for photography and video purposes.

| Taking and Editing Photos

Step 1: Launching the Camera App

Begin by unlocking your iPhone and locating the Camera app on your home screen. Tap the Camera app icon to open it.

Step 2: Understanding Camera Modes

Familiarize yourself with the various camera modes available, such as Photo, Portrait, Night, and more. Each mode caters to different shooting scenarios and provides unique features.

Step 3: Framing and Focusing

Learn to frame your shots effectively by adjusting the composition and focusing on the subject. Tap on the screen to set the focus point and adjust exposure if needed.

Step 4: Utilizing HDR

Understand how to use the HDR (High Dynamic Range) feature to capture more detailed photos, especially in challenging lighting conditions.

Step 5: Using Filters and Effects

Experiment with different filters and effects available within the Camera app to enhance the artistic quality of your photos.

Step 6: Capturing Live Photos

Discover how to take Live Photos, a feature that captures a few seconds of motion and sound before and after your shot, bringing your photos to life.

Step 7: Reviewing and Deleting Photos

Learn how to review your recently captured photos within the Camera app and delete unwanted shots to free up space on your device.

Step 8: Editing Photos

Explore the built-in editing tools to enhance your photos. Adjust exposure, contrast, color balance, and more to achieve the desired look for your images.

Recording and Sharing Videos

Step 1: Accessing the Video Mode

Switch to video mode by tapping the video camera icon within the Camera app.

Step 2: Adjusting Video Settings

Customize video settings such as resolution, frame rate, and stabilization based on your preferences and the intended use of the video.

Step 3: Holding the Phone Steady

Hold your iPhone securely to capture steady videos, reducing shakiness and enhancing the overall video quality.

Step 4: Recording Videos

Press the record button to start recording your video. Ensure a stable and smooth motion while capturing the desired content.

Step 5: Pausing and Resuming Recording

Learn how to pause and resume recording to create seamless videos, especially when capturing different scenes or segments.

Step 6: Reviewing and Trimming Videos

Access your recorded videos in the Photos app, where you can review them and trim unnecessary parts to create a polished final product.

Step 7: Sharing Videos

Understand the various ways to share your videos, including messaging, email, social media, or using cloud storage services.

| Organizing Your Media Library

Step 1: Accessing the Photos App

Open the Photos app to view and manage your photo and video library.

Step 2: Creating Albums and Folders

Organize your media by creating albums and folders to group similar photos and videos together, making it easier to find specific content.

Step 3: Using Tags and Keywords

Implement a tagging system to categorize your media further. Assign relevant keywords to aid in quick searches and organization.

Step 4: Deleting and Archiving Media

Learn how to delete unwanted photos and videos to free up space, and consider archiving valuable memories to save space without losing them.

Step 5: Backing Up Your Media

Utilize iCloud or other backup solutions to securely store your media in the cloud, ensuring you never lose precious memories.

By following these step-by-step instructions and familiarizing yourself with the iPhone 14 Pro Max's photography and video capabilities, you'll be well on your way to becoming a proficient photographer and videographer using your iPhone. Practice, explore, and unleash your creativity to capture stunning visuals and preserve cherished moments.

CHAPTER 6

SIMPLIFYING SETTINGS AND CUSTOMIZATION

I n this chapter, we will delve into the intricate world of iPhone settings and customization, aiming to simplify the process for seniors. The iPhone 14 Pro Max is a powerful device, and understanding its various settings and customization options is essential to make the most out of its features. We will cover managing preferences, personalizing your iPhone, and exploring accessibility features tailored to suit the needs of seniors.

| Managing Preferences and Settings

Setting up your iPhone

When you first get your iPhone 14 Pro Max, it's crucial to set it up correctly to suit your preferences and needs. Follow these steps to get started:

1. Press and hold the side button until the Apple logo appears.
2. Select your preferred language and region.
3. Connect to a Wi-Fi network or insert a SIM card for cellular connectivity.
4. Choose whether to set up Face ID for secure unlocking or create a passcode.
5. If you have a previous iPhone, you can restore your data and settings from an iCloud or iTunes backup.

Navigating Settings

Understanding how to navigate the iPhone's settings is fundamental for customizing your device to your liking. Here's a step-by-step guide:

1. Tap the "Settings" app icon, typically found on the home screen.
2. The Settings menu is organized into sections. Common sections include General, Display & Brightness, Sound & Haptics, Privacy, and more.
3. Within each section, you'll find submenus and various options. Tap on a specific submenu to access its settings and make adjustments.

Adjusting Display and Sound Settings

Customizing the display and sound settings can enhance your user experience:

1. **Display & Brightness**: Adjust screen brightness, text size, and enable features like True Tone.
2. **Sounds & Haptics**: Customize ringtone, vibration patterns, and adjust volume levels.

Managing Notifications and Do Not Disturb

Effectively managing notifications can help maintain a distraction-free experience:

1. **Notifications**: Customize notification settings for each app, controlling how and when you receive notifications.
2. **Do Not Disturb**: Set times when you don't want to be disturbed by calls or notifications.

Managing Battery and Power

Optimizing battery life and managing power usage is essential:

1. **Battery**: Check battery usage, enable Low Power Mode, and manage battery health.
2. **Optimizing Power Usage**: Review and manage apps that consume significant battery power.

Personalizing Your iPhone

Customizing Wallpaper and Themes

Adding a personal touch to your iPhone can be achieved by customizing the wallpaper and themes:

1. **Changing Wallpaper**: Navigate to Settings > Wallpaper > Choose a New Wallpaper to select a new wallpaper.
2. **Themes and App Icons**: Explore third-party apps that allow you to change app icons and create custom themes.

Organizing Apps and Folders

Efficiently organizing apps and creating folders can make navigation simpler:

1. **Moving and Rearranging Apps**: Press and hold an app icon to enter edit mode, then drag and drop apps to rearrange them.
2. **Creating Folders**: Drag one app icon onto another to create a folder. Name the folder and add related apps to keep your home screen organized.

Setting Up Widgets

Widgets provide quick access to information and functionalities:

1. **Adding Widgets**: Press and hold on the home screen, tap the "+" icon, and choose a widget to add.
2. **Resizing and Customizing Widgets**: Tap and hold a widget to resize or customize it according to your preference.

Accessibility Features for Seniors

Enabling Accessibility Settings

The iPhone offers a range of accessibility features to enhance usability for seniors:

1. **Accessing Accessibility Settings**: Navigate to Settings > Accessibility to explore available features.
2. **Vision Settings**: Adjust text size, display zoom, and enable features like Magnifier and VoiceOver.
3. **Hearing Settings**: Customize sound settings, enable subtitles and captions, and configure the TTY mode.

Voice Control and Siri

Voice Control and Siri can be powerful tools for seniors:

1. **Enabling Voice Control**: Navigate to Settings > Accessibility > Voice Control to set it up.
2. **Using Siri**: Activate Siri by holding the side button and ask questions or give commands using your voice.

Guided Access and Reduce Motion

These features can simplify the iPhone interface and prevent accidental actions:

1. **Guided Access**: Navigate to Settings > Accessibility > Guided Access to enable and set it up.
2. **Reduce Motion**: Navigate to Settings > Accessibility > Reduce Motion to minimize screen motion effects.

Touch Accommodations and Magnifier

Enhance touch sensitivity and utilize the magnifier feature:

1. **Touch Accommodations**: Adjust touch settings to make the screen easier to use.
2. **Magnifier**: Triple-press the side button to access the magnifier and zoom in on objects.

Mastering the art of managing preferences and settings, personalizing your iPhone, and utilizing accessibility features tailored for seniors will significantly enhance your iPhone 14 Pro Max experience. By following the step-by-step guide provided in this chapter, you'll be able to customize your device to suit your needs and preferences, making your iPhone an indispensable tool in your daily life. Remember, the key to a seamless iPhone experience is understanding and utilizing the vast array of settings and customization options at your disposal. Happy customizing!

CHAPTER 7

TROUBLESHOOTING AND TIPS

The iPhone 14 Pro Max stands as a remarkable blend of technology and user-friendliness, designed especially to cater to the unique needs of seniors. It offers a wide array of features and functionalities that enhance connectivity and convenience. However, like any sophisticated device, it may encounter occasional challenges. In this detailed chapter, we will extensively cover troubleshooting common issues, provide pro tips to optimize performance, and answer frequently asked questions. Armed with this knowledge, seniors and users will be equipped to navigate through potential roadblocks and enhance their iPhone 14 Pro Max experience.

| Common Issues and How to Resolve Them

Issue 1: Slow Performance

Step 1: Close Background Apps

One of the culprits behind a sluggish iPhone is having multiple apps running in the background. To address this, swipe up from the bottom of the screen and navigate through the open apps. Swipe up on the app's preview to close it, effectively freeing up system resources.

Step 2: Restart Your iPhone

A simple restart can work wonders in refreshing your iPhone. Press and hold the power button until "slide to power off" appears, then slide to power off. After a few seconds, press the power button again to turn it back on, which can help clear temporary files and improve performance.

Step 3: Check for Software Updates

Outdated software can often lead to performance issues. Stay up-to-date by going to Settings > General > Software Update. If there are updates available, download and install them to ensure optimal performance.

Issue 2: Connectivity Problems

Step 1: Check Network Settings

Ensure that both Wi-Fi and cellular data are turned on by navigating to Settings > Wi-Fi or Settings > Cellular. Toggle the switches if needed. If problems persist, restarting your iPhone can help apply these changes effectively.

Step 2: Forget and Reconnect to Wi-Fi

If you're facing Wi-Fi connectivity issues, navigate to Settings > Wi-Fi, tap on the Wi-Fi network, and select "Forget This Network." Reconnect by selecting the network and entering the password, which can often resolve connectivity problems.

Step 3: Reset Network Settings

For persistent network issues, resetting network settings can be a valuable solution. Go to Settings > General > Reset > Reset Network Settings. Do note that this will erase Wi-Fi passwords and cellular settings, so be prepared to re-enter them.

Issue 3: Battery Drain

Step 1: Check Battery Usage

Understanding which apps consume the most battery can help manage and optimize your iPhone's battery life. Go to Settings > Battery to view the battery usage. If any app is using an unusual amount of battery, consider limiting its usage or adjusting its settings.

Step 2: Reduce Screen Brightness

Your iPhone's screen brightness is a major factor affecting battery life. Lowering it can significantly extend the time between charges. Swipe down from the top-right corner of the screen to access Control Center and adjust the brightness slider accordingly.

Step 3: Disable Background App Refresh

To conserve battery, consider limiting the number of apps that refresh in the background. Go to Settings > General > Background App Refresh, and choose to either disable it entirely or customize it for specific apps that are essential for you.

Pro Tips for a Smoother Experience

Customize Accessibility Settings

Step 1: Enable Magnifier

For individuals with visual impairments, utilizing the Magnifier can be immensely helpful. Go to Settings > Accessibility > Magnifier and toggle the switch to enable this feature, effectively turning your iPhone into a digital magnifying glass.

Step 2: Adjust Text Size and Bold Text

To enhance readability, adjust the text size according to your preferences. Navigate to Settings > Display & Brightness > Text Size. Additionally, for bolder and clearer text, go to Settings > Display & Brightness > Bold Text.

Utilize Voice Control

Step 1: Enable Voice Control

Voice Control is a powerful tool for hands-free interaction. Navigate to Settings > Accessibility > Voice Control and toggle the switch to enable it. This feature allows you to control your iPhone using voice commands.

Step 2: Learn Voice Commands

Familiarize yourself with the numerous voice commands available with Voice Control. Simply say "Show Commands" to view a list of available commands. Learning and using these commands can significantly enhance your iPhone interaction.

Utilize Siri Shortcuts

Step 1: Set Up Siri Shortcuts

Siri Shortcuts are a fantastic way to automate routine tasks. Open the Shortcuts app, tap the "+" icon, and follow the steps to create personalized shortcuts that streamline your interactions with your iPhone.

Step 2: Use Voice Commands with Siri

Activate Siri and employ voice commands to trigger your customized Siri Shortcuts. This can save valuable time and effort, making your iPhone usage more efficient and convenient.

| Frequently Asked Questions

How Do I Take a Screenshot?

Step 1: Prepare the Screen

Navigate to the screen you wish to capture.

Step 2: Capture the Screenshot

Press the side button and the volume up button simultaneously. The screen will momentarily flash, indicating a screenshot has been successfully taken.

Step 3: Access the Screenshot

A preview of the screenshot will appear in the bottom left corner of the screen. Tap on it to access and edit the screenshot as needed.

How Do I Backup My iPhone?

Step 1: Use iCloud Backup

Ensure your data is secure by regularly backing up to iCloud. Navigate to Settings > [Your Name] > iCloud > iCloud Backup and toggle the switch to enable automatic backups. Your iPhone will back up automatically when connected to Wi-Fi and charging.

Step 2: Use iTunes/Finder Backup

For an additional layer of security, consider backing up your iPhone to your computer using iTunes (on macOS Catalina or earlier) or Finder (on macOS Big Sur and later). Connect your iPhone, select it in iTunes or Finder, click on "Backup," and choose to back up to your computer.

CHAPTER 8

DIGITAL WELL-BEING AND SECURITY

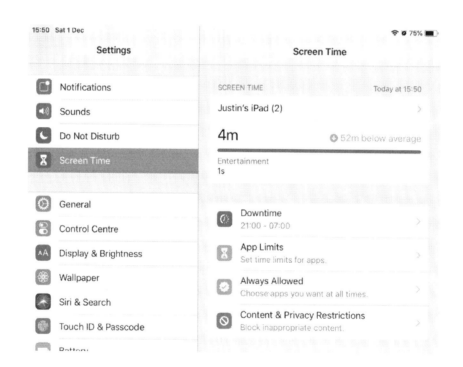

In today's digital age, smartphones have become an integral part of our lives, offering a multitude of features and functionalities. The iPhone 14 Pro Max, with its cutting-edge technology, is no exception. While this device empowers seniors with countless benefits, it also brings challenges related to digital well-being and security. In Chapter 7 of the *iPhone 14 Pro Max Seniors Guide*, we will delve into the essential aspects of maintaining a healthy digital lifestyle and securing your personal data.

| Balancing Screen Time

Understanding Screen Time

One of the key aspects of digital well-being is managing screen time effectively. The iPhone 14 Pro Max comes with a built-in feature called "Screen Time" that allows you to monitor and control the amount of time you spend on your device. To access this feature, follow these steps:

1. Open the "Settings" app on your iPhone.
2. Scroll down and tap on "Screen Time."

Once you're in the Screen Time section, you'll find a wealth of information about your device usage, including daily averages, app usage, and notifications received.

Setting App Limits

To strike a healthy balance between screen time and real-life interactions, you can set app limits for specific categories or individual apps. Here's how:

1. In the Screen Time section, tap on "App Limits."
2. Select "Add Limit" and choose a category or app you'd like to limit.
3. Set a daily time limit for the selected category or app.

Once you've set your limits, the iPhone will notify you when you're approaching the set time, helping you become more mindful of your usage.

Downtime

Downtime is a feature that allows you to schedule periods when only essential apps and phone calls are available. It's a great way to ensure you have distraction-free time for activities like reading, exercising, or spending quality time with loved ones. Here's how to set up Downtime:

1. In the Screen Time section, tap on "Downtime."
2. Set the start and end times for your Downtime.

During Downtime, you can still receive calls and access important apps, but non-essential ones will be temporarily restricted.

App Usage Reports

The iPhone 14 Pro Max provides detailed app usage reports, helping you understand which apps consume most of your time. To view these reports:

- In the Screen Time section, tap on "See All Activity" under the "Most Used" section.

By analyzing these reports, you can identify areas where you might want to cut back and allocate your time more wisely.

Turn Off Unnecessary Notifications

Excessive notifications can be a major distraction and contribute to increased screen time. To regain control over your notifications:

1. Go to "Settings."
2. Scroll down and tap on "Notifications."
3. Review the list of apps and adjust their notification settings as needed.

Consider turning off non-essential notifications or enabling the "Do Not Disturb" mode during specific hours to minimize interruptions.

Implementing Screen Time Guidelines

Establishing personal screen time guidelines can be highly beneficial. Reflect on your daily routine and commitments, and set realistic limits that align with your lifestyle. Regularly evaluate and adjust these guidelines to ensure they remain effective in promoting a healthy digital balance.

Ensuring Privacy and Security

Passcode and Face ID

Protecting your iPhone's physical security is paramount. The iPhone 14 Pro Max offers two primary security features: Passcode and Face ID.

Passcode:

A passcode is a numeric or alphanumeric code that unlocks your device. To set or change your passcode, go to "Settings" > "Face ID & Passcode" (or "Touch ID & Passcode" if your device has Touch ID). Here, you can enable or change your passcode.

Face ID:

Face ID uses facial recognition technology to unlock your phone. It's secure and convenient. To set up Face ID, navigate to "Settings" > "Face ID & Passcode," and follow the on-screen instructions.

Two-Factor Authentication

Two-factor authentication (2FA) adds an extra layer of security to your Apple ID, protecting your personal information. To enable 2FA:

1. Open "Settings."
2. Tap on your Apple ID at the top of the screen.
3. Select "Password & Security."
4. Tap on "Turn On Two-Factor Authentication" and follow the prompts.

With 2FA enabled, even if someone knows your password, they won't be able to access your Apple ID without the second verification step.

App Permissions

Your iPhone grants apps access to various features and data, such as your location, camera, and microphone. It's crucial to review and manage these permissions to protect your privacy.

1. Go to "Settings." b.
2. Scroll down and select an app.
3. Review and adjust its permissions as needed.

Regularly review the permissions you've granted to ensure they align with the app's purpose and your privacy preferences.

Safari Privacy Settings

Safari, the default web browser on your iPhone, offers several privacy features:

a. **Prevent Cross-Site Tracking:** In "Settings" > "Safari," enable "Prevent Cross-Site Tracking" to limit advertisers from tracking your online behavior.

b. **Block All Cookies:** You can choose to block all cookies or allow them only from websites you visit. This setting is also in "Settings" > "Safari" > "Privacy & Security."

c. **Fraudulent Website Warning:** Enable "Fraudulent Website Warning" to be alerted if you visit a suspected phishing site.

d. **Search Engine and Privacy:** You can change your default search engine to one that prioritizes privacy, such as DuckDuckGo, in "Settings" > "Safari" > "Search Engine."

App Store Security

Installing apps from the App Store is generally safe, but it's still essential to be cautious:

a. Only download apps from reputable developers.
b. Read user reviews and check for any red flags.
c. Avoid sideloading apps from unverified sources, as this can pose security risks.

Additionally, regularly update your apps to ensure you have the latest security patches.

Find My iPhone

In case your iPhone is lost or stolen, the "Find My" app can help you locate it or remotely erase your data to prevent unauthorized access. To set up Find My iPhone:

1. Open "Settings."
2. Tap on your Apple ID.
3. Select "Find My."
4. Turn on "Find My iPhone."

You can also enable "Send Last Location" to help you locate your device even if the battery is critically low.

Enhancing Digital Well-Being

Night Shift and True Tone

The iPhone 14 Pro Max offers features like Night Shift and True Tone to reduce eye strain and improve digital well-being:

a. **Night Shift:** This feature adjusts the colors on your display to the warmer end of the spectrum during the evening. To enable Night Shift, go to "Settings" > "Display & Brightness" > "Night Shift."

b. **True Tone:** True Tone adapts the display to the ambient light, making the screen more comfortable on your eyes. You can enable it in "Settings" > "Display & Brightness" > "True Tone."

Accessibility Features

The iPhone 14 Pro Max includes a range of accessibility features that can enhance your digital experience and well-being:

a. **Magnifier:** The Magnifier app turns your iPhone into a magnifying glass, making it easier to read small text. To use it, go to "Settings" > "Accessibility" > "Magnifier" and turn it on.

b. **Text Size and Bold Text:** Adjust text size and enable bold text in "Settings" > "Display & Brightness" > "Text Size" or "Bold Text" to improve readability.

c. **Reduce Motion:** To reduce motion effects, which can be helpful if you experience motion sickness, go to "Settings" > "Accessibility" > "Motion" and turn on "Reduce Motion."

Mindfulness and Health Apps

To enhance your digital well-being, consider utilizing mindfulness and health apps available on the App Store. These apps can guide you through meditation, breathing exercises, and physical activities to help you relax and maintain a healthy lifestyle.

GETTING HELP AND SUPPORT

Welcome to Chapter 9 of the iPhone 14 Pro Max Senior's Guide. In this chapter, we will explore the essential aspects of getting help and support when you encounter issues with your device. Apple products, including the iPhone 14 Pro Max, are known for their user-friendly interfaces and robust performance. However, it's natural to face questions or challenges as you explore the various features of your device. To ensure a seamless experience, it's crucial to know how to access user guides, utilize available resources, contact Apple Support, and troubleshoot common problems with confidence. This chapter will be your go-to resource for all things related to seeking help and support for your iPhone 14 Pro Max.

Accessing User Guides and Resources

The iPhone 14 Pro Max comes with a plethora of features, and it's important to have access to comprehensive user guides and resources to make the most of your device. Here's how you can do it step by step:

Step 1: Open the Apple Books App

The Apple Books app is your gateway to accessing user guides and resources for your iPhone. It's pre-installed on your device, and you can find it on your home screen. Look for the icon with an open book.

Step 2: Search for the User Guide

Once you've opened the Apple Books app, tap on the "Search" tab at the bottom right corner. In the search bar, type "iPhone 14 Pro Max User Guide" and press "Search."

Step 3: Download the User Guide

The search results will display the official user guide for the iPhone 14 Pro Max. Tap on it to open the book. You'll see options to "Get" or "Buy" the guide. Since it's an official resource, you can tap "Get" to download it for free.

Step 4: Accessing the User Guide

After the download is complete, tap on the book cover to open the user guide. You can now browse through the guide to find information on various features, settings, and tips for using your iPhone 14 Pro Max.

Step 5: Utilizing Interactive Features

Apple user guides often contain interactive features like links and videos. You can tap on these elements to get more detailed information or watch instructional videos right from the user guide.

Step 6: Use the Search Function

If you're looking for specific information, use the search function within the user guide. Tap the magnifying glass icon, enter your query, and the guide will show you relevant sections.

Contacting Apple Support

Sometimes, you may encounter issues with your iPhone that can't be resolved by simply reading the user guide. In such cases, it's essential to know how to contact Apple Support. Here's a step-by-step guide:

Step 1: Open the Settings App

Begin by navigating to the Settings app on your iPhone 14 Pro Max. You can find it on your home screen, typically represented by a gear icon.

Step 2: Scroll Down and Select "Support"

In the Settings app, scroll down to find the "Support" option. It's usually located in the section with various Apple-related options.

Step 3: Tap on "Contact Apple Support"

Under the "Support" section, tap on "Contact Apple Support." This will initiate the process of reaching out to Apple's support team.

Step 4: Choose the Issue You're Facing

You'll be presented with a list of common issues. Select the one that best matches your problem. If your issue isn't listed, you can still proceed by selecting a related topic.

Step 5: Contact Options

Depending on your selected issue, you'll be given options for contacting Apple Support. These options may include "Chat," "Call," or "Schedule a Call." Choose the one that suits your preference.

Step 6: Follow the Prompts

Once you've selected your preferred contact method, follow the on-screen prompts. If you choose to chat or schedule a call, you'll be prompted to provide details about your issue and preferred contact time. If you opt to call, the iPhone will initiate the call for you.

Step 7: Communicate with Apple Support

You'll now be connected with an Apple Support representative who will guide you through troubleshooting steps or offer assistance with your issue. Be sure to provide them with all relevant information about the problem you're facing.

Troubleshooting with Confidence

Troubleshooting common issues is an essential skill for any iPhone user. Here's how you can confidently troubleshoot problems with your iPhone 14 Pro Max:

Step 1: Identify the Problem

The first step in troubleshooting is to identify the problem accurately. Is it a hardware issue, a software glitch, or a user error? Take note of any error messages or unusual behavior to help pinpoint the issue.

Step 2: Restart Your iPhone

Many problems can be resolved by simply restarting your iPhone. To do this, press and hold the power button until the "slide to power off" slider appears. Slide it to turn off your device and then press and hold the power button again to turn it back on.

Step 3: Check for Software Updates

Outdated software can lead to various issues. Ensure that your iPhone's operating system is up to date by going to Settings > General > Software Update. If an update is available, tap "Download and Install."

Step 4: Reset Settings

If your iPhone is experiencing persistent issues, you can try resetting your settings. Go to Settings > General > Reset > Reset All Settings. This will reset your device's settings to their default values, but your data will remain intact.

Step 5: Backup and Restore

If all else fails, you may need to perform a backup and restore. Connect your iPhone to a computer and use iTunes or Finder to create a backup. Then, go to Settings > General > Reset > Erase All Content and Settings. After the reset, you can restore your data from the backup.

Step 6: Seek Professional Help

If the problem persists after trying the above steps, it's time to seek professional help. Contact Apple Support as described in Section 2 or visit an Apple Store or authorized service provider for hardware issues.

CHAPTER 10

STAYING CONNECTED WITH LOVED ONES

In an increasingly digital age, staying connected with loved ones has become an integral part of our daily lives. The iPhone 14 Pro Max, with its advanced features and user-friendly interface, offers seniors a powerful tool to connect with family and friends, share precious moments, and ensure online safety. In this chapter, we will delve deep into the ways seniors can leverage the capabilities of the iPhone 14 Pro Max to foster and maintain meaningful connections, navigate the world of digital communication with ease, and safeguard their online experiences.

| Connecting with Family and Friends

The Importance of Staying Connected

As we age, maintaining relationships with family and friends becomes even more crucial for our emotional well-being. Isolation and loneliness can have detrimental effects on senior citizens, both mentally and physically. The iPhone 14 Pro Max can be a lifeline, allowing seniors to bridge the gap between physical distances and stay emotionally close to their loved ones.

Making Calls

The most fundamental way to connect with family and friends is through voice calls. The iPhone 14 Pro Max boasts crystal-clear call quality, making it easier for seniors to have meaningful conversations.

1. To make a call, simply tap the Phone app, select a contact, and press the green call button.
2. For seniors who might have difficulty typing, Siri, Apple's voice assistant, can be activated with a simple "Hey Siri" command, making hands-free calling a breeze.

Video Calls

While voice calls are great, nothing beats the warmth of seeing a loved one's face. Video calls, facilitated by apps like FaceTime and Zoom, allow seniors to have virtual face-to-face conversations. With the iPhone 14 Pro Max's high-quality camera and sharp display, these video calls can feel almost as good as being there in person. We'll explore the specifics of making video calls and using these apps in later sections.

Messaging

Text messaging is another convenient way to stay in touch. Seniors can send text messages, photos, and videos to family and friends, creating a continuous flow of communication. The Messages app on the iPhone 14 Pro Max offers various features, including the ability to send voice messages and share your location, making it even more versatile for staying connected.

FaceTime: Connecting Through Video Calls

FaceTime is Apple's native video calling app, and it's designed to be user-friendly for seniors. Here's a step-by-step guide on how to use FaceTime on your iPhone 14 Pro Max:

Step 1: Open FaceTime

To start a FaceTime call, open the FaceTime app on your iPhone 14 Pro Max. You can find it by swiping down on the home screen and searching for "FaceTime" or by locating it in your app library.

Step 2: Sign In

If you're not already signed in, you'll need to do so using your Apple ID. This ensures that you can make and receive FaceTime calls with your contacts.

Step 3: Select a Contact

Tap the "+" icon to add a contact to your FaceTime list. You can either enter a contact's name or phone number or select someone from your contacts.

Step 4: Make the Call

Once you've selected a contact, tap their name, and then tap the video camera icon to initiate a video call. Alternatively, you can start an audio-only call by tapping the phone icon.

Step 5: Enjoy the Call

During your FaceTime call, you can switch between the front and rear cameras, mute your microphone, and adjust the volume. To end the call, simply tap the red "End" button.

Zoom: Expanding Your Video Communication Options

Zoom is another popular app for video calls, especially for group meetings and virtual gatherings. Here's how seniors can use Zoom on their iPhone 14 Pro Max:

Step 1: Download Zoom

If you don't already have the Zoom app, you can download it from the App Store. Search for "Zoom Cloud Meetings" and install the app.

Step 2: Sign In or Create an Account

Launch the Zoom app and sign in with your Zoom account if you have one. If not, you can create a free account.

Step 3: Start or Join a Meeting

To start a new meeting, tap the "New Meeting" button and select your preferences. To join an existing meeting, tap "Join" and enter the meeting ID provided by the host.

Step 4: Adjust Settings

Before or during a meeting, you can adjust your camera, microphone, and speaker settings. Zoom also allows you to share your screen if needed.

Step 5: End the Meeting

When the meeting is over, tap "Leave" to exit. You'll have the option to end the meeting for all participants or leave while the meeting continues.

| Sharing Moments with Ease

Photos and Videos

One of the joys of staying connected with loved ones is sharing precious moments. With the iPhone 14 Pro Max's remarkable camera capabilities, seniors can capture high-quality photos and videos to share with family and friends. Here's how to make the most of it:

Taking Photos and Videos

1. Open the Camera app, frame your shot, and press the shutter button to take a photo or start recording a video.
2. Use the various camera modes available, such as Portrait mode for stunning portraits and Night mode for low-light photography.
3. Experiment with camera settings like exposure, focus, and HDR to improve your photography skills.

Organizing Your Media

1. Your photos and videos are automatically organized in the Photos app. You can create albums, add captions, and sort your media for easy access.
2. Use the Memories feature to relive your favorite moments through automatically generated slideshows.

Sharing Media

1. To share a photo or video, open it in the Photos app, tap the share button (a square with an arrow pointing up), and select how you want to share it (via text message, email, social media, etc.).
2. You can also create shared albums to collaborate on photo collections with friends and family.

Social Media

Social media platforms like Facebook, Instagram, and Twitter provide seniors with the means to share updates, photos, and videos with a wider circle of friends and relatives. The iPhone 14 Pro Max makes using these platforms simple:

Setting Up Social Media Accounts

1. Download the respective social media apps from the App Store.
2. Sign in to your existing account or create a new one.
3. Customize your profile with a profile picture, bio, and personal information.

Posting Updates

1. Open the social media app of your choice.
2. Tap the "+" or "Create" button to start a new post.
3. You can share text updates, photos, videos, and even live streams.

Connecting with Friends

1. Use the search feature to find and follow your friends and family on social media.
2. Interact with their posts by liking, commenting, or sharing.

Privacy Settings

1. Ensure your privacy by adjusting settings for who can see your posts, who can send you friend requests, and who can comment on your content.

Email

Email remains a versatile and reliable method of communication, especially for sharing longer messages, documents, or links. Seniors can easily set up and use email on their iPhone 14 Pro Max:

Setting Up an Email Account

2. Open the Mail app on your iPhone 14 Pro Max.
3. Tap "Add Account" and select your email service provider (e.g., Gmail, Yahoo, Outlook).
4. Follow the on-screen instructions to sign in and configure your email account.

Composing and Sending Emails

1. Tap the compose button (usually a pencil icon) to start a new email.
2. Enter the recipient's email address, subject, and compose your message.
3. You can attach photos, videos, and documents by tapping the paperclip icon.
4. Hit "Send" when you're ready to send the email.

Managing Email

1. Keep your inbox organized by creating folders or labels to sort and categorize your emails.
2. Mark important emails as unread, flag them for follow-up, or move them to designated folders.

| Online Safety for Seniors

The Importance of Online Safety

Navigating the digital world safely is a paramount concern, especially for seniors. The internet offers tremendous benefits, but it's crucial to be aware of potential risks and how to protect yourself. The iPhone 14 Pro Max offers several features to enhance online safety for seniors.

Passcode and Biometrics

Protecting your iPhone with a strong passcode or biometric authentication (such as Face ID or Touch ID) is the first line of defense against unauthorized access. Here's how to set up a passcode and biometrics on your iPhone 14 Pro Max:

Setting Up a Passcode

1. Go to "Settings" > "Face ID & Passcode" (or "Touch ID & Passcode" if your device has Touch ID).
2. Tap "Turn Passcode On" and follow the prompts to create a passcode.

Setting Up Face ID

1. Go to "Settings" > "Face ID & Passcode."
2. Tap "Enroll Face" and follow the on-screen instructions to set up Face ID.

Setting Up Touch ID

1. Go to "Settings" > "Touch ID & Passcode."
2. Follow the instructions to set up Touch ID by scanning your fingerprint.

App Permissions

Be mindful of the permissions you grant to apps on your iPhone 14 Pro Max. Only allow access to essential features and information. Here's how to manage app permissions:

Managing App Permissions

1. Go to "Settings" > "Privacy" to see a list of permissions organized by type (e.g., Camera, Contacts, Location).
2. Tap on a permission to review which apps have access and toggle them on or off as needed.

Phishing and Suspicious Messages

Seniors are often targeted by phishing attempts through email, text messages, or phone calls. It's crucial to recognize and avoid suspicious communications. Here are some tips:

Identifying Phishing Attempts

- Be cautious of unsolicited communications asking for personal or financial information.
- Check for misspellings, generic greetings, and suspicious URLs in emails or messages.
- Do not click on links or download attachments from unknown or suspicious sources.

Reporting Suspicious Messages

- If you receive a suspicious message, report it to your email or messaging service to help prevent further attempts.

Staying connected with loved ones, sharing life's moments, and ensuring online safety are central aspects of a fulfilling digital experience for seniors using the iPhone 14 Pro Max. With this powerful device and the insights provided in this chapter, seniors can navigate the world of digital communication confidently, cherishing their relationships and engaging with the online world securely. Harness the potential of the iPhone 14 Pro Max to connect, share, and stay safe in the modern era of technology.

CHAPTER 11

MASTERING IOS UPADES

In the fast-paced world of technology, staying up-to-date with the latest software updates is essential, especially when you're using a cutting-edge device like the iPhone 14 Pro Max. Apple consistently releases new iOS updates, each packed with exciting features and essential security enhancements. In Chapter 9, we delve into the art of mastering iOS updates. This comprehensive guide aims to help seniors make the most out of their iPhone 14 Pro Max by ensuring that they are always running the latest iOS version, understanding the new features it brings, and offering tips for a seamless updating experience.

Keeping Your Device Up-to-Date

Your iPhone 14 Pro Max, like all electronic devices, requires regular software updates to maintain its performance, security, and functionality. Keeping your device up-to-date is crucial for several reasons, and this section will explore why and how you should do it.

The Importance of iOS Updates

iOS updates are not just about flashy new features; they play a vital role in the overall health and performance of your iPhone. Here's why they matter:

Security Enhancements

Apple continually identifies and fixes security vulnerabilities in each iOS update. By keeping your device updated, you protect yourself from potential threats like malware, data breaches, and identity theft. Seniors, who are often targeted by online scams, will benefit greatly from these security enhancements.

Improved Performance

iOS updates also come with performance improvements. Apple fine-tunes its operating system to run more smoothly and efficiently on your iPhone 14 Pro Max. This means faster app loading, smoother multitasking, and overall better performance.

Bug Fixes

Software is not perfect, and bugs can surface over time. iOS updates address these issues, ensuring that your device functions as intended. Common problems like app crashes, freezing, or unexpected shutdowns can often be resolved with an update.

Compatibility

Staying up-to-date ensures that your iPhone 14 Pro Max remains compatible with the latest apps and services. Older iOS versions may not support some of the newer applications, limiting your device's functionality.

How to Update Your iPhone 14 Pro Max

Now that we've established the importance of iOS updates, let's go over the steps to keep your device up-to-date.

Automatic Updates

Apple makes it easy to keep your device current by offering automatic updates. To enable this feature, go to "Settings," then "General," and select "Software Update." Here, you can turn on "Download iOS updates" and "Install iOS updates" to have your device automatically update when connected to Wi-Fi and charging.

Manual Updates

If you prefer a more hands-on approach or want to ensure updates are installed at a convenient time, you can manually update your iPhone 14 Pro Max. To do this, go to "Settings," then "General," and tap "Software Update." If an update is available, you'll see an option to "Download and Install." Follow the on-screen instructions to complete the process.

Checking for Updates

If you want to check for updates without enabling automatic downloads, you can periodically visit the "Software Update" section in "Settings." Here, you can see if any updates are available and choose to download and install them.

Understanding New iOS Features

iOS updates not only enhance security and performance but also introduce exciting new features and improvements. It's essential to understand these changes to make the most of your iPhone 14 Pro Max. In this section, we'll delve into some of the latest iOS features seniors should be aware of.

The Control Center Revamp

Apple often tweaks the Control Center in iOS updates to provide better access to essential functions. With the iPhone 14 Pro Max, you'll find a redesigned Control Center that makes it easier to adjust settings like screen brightness, volume, and music playback. This feature is particularly useful for seniors who may prefer larger icons and simplified controls.

Focus Mode

Focus Mode is a new addition to iOS that helps you concentrate on specific tasks or activities by filtering notifications. Seniors can benefit from this feature by customizing Focus Modes for different scenarios, such as reading, driving, or relaxation. This ensures that only relevant notifications reach you, reducing distractions.

FaceTime Improvements

FaceTime has become an integral part of staying connected, especially for seniors who may be geographically distant from family and friends. iOS updates often bring enhancements to FaceTime, including improved video and audio quality, spatial audio for a more immersive experience, and FaceTime Links for scheduling and sharing calls. These features make FaceTime more accessible and enjoyable for seniors.

Enhanced Privacy Features

Privacy is a growing concern in the digital age, and Apple takes it seriously. Each iOS update typically includes new privacy features to protect your personal data. Seniors can take advantage of these features to safeguard their information online. Recent additions like App Privacy Reports and Mail Privacy Protection give you more control over your digital footprint.

Redesigned Notifications

iOS updates often refine the notification system, making it easier to manage incoming alerts. Seniors can appreciate these improvements, as they help declutter the notification center and make it simpler to prioritize messages, emails, and other notifications.

Health App Enhancements

The Health app on your iPhone 14 Pro Max is a valuable tool for tracking your well-being. iOS updates regularly expand its capabilities, providing seniors with more options for monitoring their health and fitness. Features like Trends, Mobility Metrics, and Health Sharing empower you to take charge of your health.

| Tips for Seamless Updates

While updating your iPhone's operating system is essential, it can sometimes be a daunting task. In this section, we'll share some tips and best practices to ensure that the update process goes smoothly for seniors.

Back Up Your Device

Before initiating any iOS update, it's crucial to back up your iPhone 14 Pro Max. This ensures that your data, including photos, contacts, and app settings, is safe in case anything goes wrong during the update. You can back up your device using iCloud or iTunes on a computer.

Ensure Sufficient Storage

iOS updates can be quite substantial, often requiring several gigabytes of free storage space. Before downloading an update, check your available storage and remove unnecessary apps, photos, or files to make room for the update.

Use Wi-Fi

Downloading iOS updates over a Wi-Fi connection is recommended, as it ensures a stable and faster download process. Mobile data can be used, but it may consume a significant amount of your data plan.

Update Overnight

If you're concerned about the update process disrupting your daily activities, consider scheduling it for overnight installation. Your iPhone can automatically install updates while you sleep, ensuring minimal disruption.

Keep Your Passcode Handy

During the update, your iPhone may ask for your passcode. Ensure you remember it or have it written down in a safe place. This step is essential to complete the installation.

Stay Patient

iOS updates can take some time to download and install, depending on your internet speed and the size of the update. It's crucial to be patient and allow the process to complete without interruption.

Mastering iOS updates on your iPhone 14 Pro Max is an essential part of ensuring a smooth and secure user experience. Keeping your device up-to-date, understanding new iOS features, and following best practices for seamless updates will empower you to make the most of your iPhone's capabilities. Stay informed, stay secure, and enjoy all that your iPhone 14 Pro Max has to offer.

CHAPTER 12

PRACTICAL APPLICATIONS FOR DAILY LIFE

The iPhone 14 Pro Max is a technological marvel that has not only revolutionized the way we communicate but has also become an indispensable tool in our daily lives. For seniors, this device offers a plethora of features that can significantly enhance their quality of life and make routine activities more convenient. In this chapter, we will delve into practical applications of the iPhone 14 Pro Max for seniors, focusing on GPS and maps, mobile payments, and shopping. We will explore how seniors can leverage these features to navigate the world around them, manage finances, and simplify shopping experiences.

Using iPhone in Practical Situations

The iPhone, with its cutting-edge technology and versatile features, has become an integral part of our daily lives, profoundly impacting the way we interact, work, and navigate the world. For seniors, the iPhone can be a powerful tool to simplify and enhance various practical situations, promoting independence, connectivity, and convenience. In this section, we will explore how the iPhone can be utilized effectively in practical scenarios that seniors commonly encounter.

Communication and Social Connectivity

The iPhone serves as a vital tool for communication, enabling seniors to stay in touch with family, friends, and healthcare providers. Phone calls, text messages, emails, and video calls can all be easily managed through the iPhone's user-friendly interface. Seniors can communicate with loved ones irrespective of geographic distances, combating feelings of isolation and fostering social connectivity.

Additionally, social media platforms like Facebook and WhatsApp have user-friendly iPhone applications that facilitate easy interaction with friends and family. Seniors can share updates, photos, and engage in conversations, promoting a sense of community and staying informed about the lives of their loved ones.

Health and Well-being

The iPhone offers a multitude of health-related applications that can aid seniors in managing their well-being. Health and fitness apps can help track daily activities, monitor vital signs, manage medications, and even provide guided exercises. With features like the Health app, seniors can keep a comprehensive record of their health data, making it easier to share vital information with healthcare professionals during appointments.

Moreover, the iPhone can be used to access telehealth services, allowing seniors to consult healthcare providers from the comfort of their homes. This is especially beneficial for those with mobility challenges or living in remote areas, ensuring they receive timely medical advice and care.

Emergency Assistance

The iPhone serves as a safety net for seniors in case of emergencies. The device allows them to call for help swiftly by utilizing the Emergency SOS feature, which, when activated, can automatically dial emergency services and notify designated contacts about the situation and location. This provides a sense of security and assurance to both seniors and their loved ones.

Additionally, medical ID information can be set up on the iPhone, providing crucial details about allergies, medications, and existing health conditions. In an emergency, first responders can access this information even if the iPhone is locked, enabling them to provide appropriate medical care.

Information and Learning

The iPhone opens up a world of knowledge and learning opportunities for seniors. With access to the internet and a plethora of educational apps, seniors can engage in lifelong learning, from learning new languages to exploring hobbies or understanding the latest news and advancements. The iPhone's intuitive search capabilities and the availability of eBooks enable seniors to delve into a vast array of topics at their own pace and interest.

Personal Organization and Reminders

The iPhone can act as a powerful personal organizer for seniors, helping them keep track of appointments, to-do lists, birthdays, and important events. The built-in Calendar app, Notes app, and Reminders app are excellent tools to maintain a structured and organized schedule. Seniors can set reminders for medications, appointments, or any other daily tasks, ensuring they stay on top of their responsibilities and commitments.

Furthermore, voice assistants like Siri can be utilized to set reminders, make calls, send messages, or even inquire about the weather using simple voice commands. This hands-free functionality enhances accessibility and ease of use, especially for seniors with limited dexterity or mobility.

Financial Management

The iPhone offers a range of applications and features that enable seniors to manage their finances efficiently. Mobile banking apps allow easy access to bank accounts, bill payments, and budget tracking. Additionally, financial management apps can provide insights into spending patterns, helping seniors make informed financial decisions and budget effectively.

The integration of Apple Pay and digital wallet applications allows seniors to make secure transactions, both online and in stores, without the need for physical cash or cards. This not only streamlines the payment process but also enhances security by minimizing the risk of theft or loss of physical belongings.

Travel and Navigation

Whether seniors are traveling locally or planning a trip, the iPhone's GPS and map features can be invaluable. The Maps application provides accurate directions, real-time traffic updates, and points of interest, making navigation seamless and stress-free. Seniors can confidently explore new places, find nearby restaurants, and plan their journeys with ease, enhancing their travel experiences.

Furthermore, language translation apps and currency converters can be incredibly useful when traveling internationally, ensuring effective communication and financial understanding in diverse regions.

GPS and Maps for Seniors

Navigating the World with Ease

One of the remarkable features of the iPhone 14 Pro Max is its advanced GPS capabilities, making it an ideal companion for seniors who may require assistance with navigation. The device offers precise location tracking and real-time directions, making it easier for seniors to travel confidently, whether by foot, public transport, or car.

The built-in Apple Maps application provides detailed maps, turn-by-turn directions, and real-time traffic updates. Seniors can simply input their destination and follow the instructions provided, ensuring a smooth and stress-free journey. The large, high-resolution display of the iPhone 14 Pro Max enhances readability, making it easier for seniors to view maps and directions without straining their eyes.

Location Sharing for Safety and Convenience

For seniors, safety is of paramount importance, especially when navigating unfamiliar areas. The iPhone 14 Pro Max offers a feature that allows users to share their real-time location with family members or trusted individuals. This can be immensely beneficial for seniors who may want to keep loved ones informed about their whereabouts, providing peace of mind to both seniors and their families.

In the event of an emergency or if assistance is needed, the ability to quickly share one's location with a trusted contact can be a lifesaver. This feature adds an extra layer of security and ensures that help can be summoned promptly if required.

Exploring Nearby Places of Interest

The iPhone 14 Pro Max enables seniors to explore their surroundings effortlessly. Using the Maps application, seniors can search for nearby places of interest, such as restaurants, parks, hospitals, and more. Detailed information, including reviews and ratings, is readily available, allowing seniors to make informed choices about where to go and what activities to engage in.

This feature can be particularly valuable for seniors who are looking to discover new places, socialize, or engage in recreational activities. It encourages an active lifestyle and helps seniors stay connected with their communities.

Mobile Payments and Shopping

Streamlining Finances with Mobile Payments

The iPhone 14 Pro Max offers a secure and convenient platform for mobile payments, revolutionizing the way we handle financial transactions. For seniors, this feature can be a game-changer, allowing them to manage their finances with ease and confidence.

With Apple Pay and other mobile payment apps, seniors can link their credit or debit cards to their iPhone and make payments swiftly and securely. The process is simple and involves just a few taps on the screen. This eliminates the need for carrying physical wallets and reduces the risk of loss or theft of cash or cards.

Enhancing Shopping Experiences

The iPhone 14 Pro Max elevates the shopping experience for seniors, offering a host of applications and features that allow for seamless online shopping. Seniors can explore a vast array of products and services, compare prices, read reviews, and make purchases without leaving the comfort of their homes.

Online shopping apps like Amazon, eBay, and various retail store apps offer seniors a user-friendly interface and intuitive navigation, ensuring a hassle-free shopping experience. The iPhone's large screen and clear display further enhance the shopping process, making it easy for seniors to browse and select items.

Accessibility Features for Shopping

Apple has always been at the forefront of providing accessibility features to cater to diverse user needs. Seniors with specific accessibility requirements can customize their iPhone 14 Pro Max to suit their preferences, making shopping and using mobile payment apps even more user-friendly.

Features such as VoiceOver, Magnifier, Larger Text, and Speech make it easier for seniors to read product descriptions, view details, and complete transactions. These accessibility features are a testament to Apple's commitment to ensuring that all users, including seniors, can fully utilize the capabilities of their devices.

The iPhone 14 Pro Max is a remarkable device that has the power to significantly impact the lives of seniors. Its features, including advanced GPS and maps capabilities, mobile payment options, and seamless shopping experiences, are designed to enhance convenience, safety, and overall well-being. By leveraging these features, seniors can navigate the world around them with confidence, manage their finances securely, and enjoy a more accessible and streamlined shopping process. The iPhone 14 Pro Max is more than just a smartphone; it is a valuable tool that empowers seniors to embrace technology and live life to the fullest.

CHAPTER 13

ENJOYING A SIMPLIFIED DIGITAL LIFESTYLE

In an age where technology is rapidly advancing and becoming an integral part of our lives, embracing the digital realm can sometimes feel overwhelming, especially for seniors. However, the iPhone 14 Pro Max, with its user-friendly interface and intuitive features, presents an opportunity for seniors to not only adapt to but also enjoy a simplified digital lifestyle. This chapter delves into achieving digital independence, seamlessly integrating technology into daily life, and staying engaged and informed with the aid of iPhone 14 Pro Max.

Achieving Digital Independence

The iPhone 14 Pro Max offers numerous features that can help seniors achieve digital independence and confidently use their devices. Understanding and utilizing features like Face ID for secure unlocking, Siri for voice commands, VoiceOver for screen reading, and Accessibility settings to customize the interface are key for simplified use.

Face ID allows seniors to unlock their phone and authorize purchases simply by looking at the device, eliminating the need to remember passcodes. Siri enables voice control of calls, texts, calendar, music and more, reducing reliance on complex touch gestures. VoiceOver reads onscreen text aloud while Magnifier enlarges it for those with visual impairments. Adjusting text size, display colors, and touch accommodations in Settings further optimizes accessibility. With practice, these features provide seniors with seamless phone operation.

Navigating the User Interface

Becoming familiar with the iPhone 14 Pro Max's user interface is essential for seniors to interact with their device comfortably. The home screen contains apps and widgets that can be organized based on usage frequency and preference. Swiping left reveals additional home screens for more apps. The dock at the bottom provides one-touch access to your most used apps. Touching and holding an app icon allows adjusting, deleting or repositioning it.

The Control Center accessed by swiping down from the top right corner contains frequently used settings like Wi-Fi, Bluetooth, Flashlight and an iOS Media player. Swiping up from the bottom edge reveals all your open apps to easily switch between them. Touch ID or Face ID allow swift unlocking and app authorization. Gestures like swiping, scrolling, zooming, tapping and pressing grow intuitive with practice. Customizing sounds, text size, wallpaper and Siri commands in Settings helps create an interface tailored to the senior's needs and preferences for optimal usability.

Communication and Social Interaction

The iPhone 14 Pro Max provides multiple means for seniors to communicate with loved ones and stay socially engaged. Making audio or FaceTime video calls enables speaking face-to-face. iMessage allows instant text conversations with other Apple users including photos, stickers and more. Third-party apps like WhatsApp or Facebook Messenger can text non-iPhone contacts.

Built-in apps like Mail, Contacts and Calendar help seniors stay organized and connected. Social media apps like Facebook and Instagram let users share life updates, photos/videos and interact with family and friends. Events, Reminders and Notes keep important occasions and tasks in focus. By fully utilizing these communication and social features on the iPhone 14 Pro Max, seniors can nurture relationships and maintain an active social life from anywhere.

Managing Health and Wellness

The iPhone 14 Pro Max contains Apple's Health app which can aid seniors in monitoring and optimizing their health and wellness. Users can track vitals like sleep, steps, heart rate, blood pressure, blood glucose, medications, pain, mobility and more. Health data can be shared with caregivers or doctors for better care collaboration. The Fitness app provides guided workouts, activity rings and fitness tracker integration to encourage an active lifestyle. Mindfulness and meditation apps like Calm promote mental health through breathing, sleep and relaxation exercises. By embracing these apps, seniors can utilize their iPhone to manage medical care, improve fitness and reduce stress for optimal wellbeing.

Exploring Hobbies and Leisure

Thanks to the 2 million+ apps on the App Store, the iPhone 14 Pro Max allows seniors to explore endless hobbies and leisure activities from their device. Photography apps unleash creativity and allow editing and organizing photos. Digital books, magazines and audiobooks from Apple Books provide unlimited reading material. Gardening, cooking and DIY apps assist with new skills acquisition. Games and puzzles exercise the mind, while education and language learning apps facilitate continued development. Virtual museum tours and travel apps enable cultural exploration from home. The possibilities are vast for seniors to pursue their interests and passions right from their iPhone.

Accessing News and Information

Staying current and accessing endless information is easily achievable for seniors using their iPhone 14 Pro Max. The Apple News app delivers personalized news curated to the reader's interests, while News+ provides unlimited access to premium magazines and newspapers. Podcasts allow users to subscribe to audio shows on topics they enjoy. Kindle and Audible provide millions of ebooks and audiobooks. Informational apps like Wikipedia and Google contain a wealth of constantly updated knowledge. This 24/7 education and news access empowers seniors to stay engaged with the world.

Learning and Education

The iPhone 14 Pro Max grants seniors exceptional opportunities for continued learning and education. Apps like LinkedIn Learning, Udemy and Coursera provide online video courses taught by experts on every topic imaginable. Apps Babbel, Duolingo and Rosetta Stone facilitate foreign language acquisition. Educational podcasts deliver lessons and lectures from world-class institutions. Kindle books provide limitless reading material. Seniors can even attend live university classes remotely through Outschool. By tapping these resources, seniors can become lifelong learners and expand their knowledge from the convenience of their iPhone.

Enhancing Travel and Exploration

For seniors with a passion for travel and new experiences, the iPhone 14 Pro Max can significantly enrich these pursuits. Apps like Google Maps, Waze, Tripadvisor and AirBnB allow planning personalized adventures. Language translation apps facilitate communication abroad, while airline and hotel apps organize bookings. Location-based Yelp reviews help discover local hotspots. Google Lens translates text and identifies landmarks in real-time via camera. The iPhone provides all the tools needed to simplify navigation, spotlight bucket-list destinations, book affordable travel and immerse in foreign cultures for remarkable senior adventures.

FAQ

Q 1: What are the basics of using the iPhone 14 Pro Max, and how do I get started with it?

The iPhone 14 Pro Max is an advanced smartphone designed to provide a seamless user experience. To get started, press and hold the power button on the right side of the device until the Apple logo appears. Follow the on-screen prompts to set up your language, region, Wi-Fi, and Apple ID. Once the initial setup is complete, you're ready to explore the device.

Q 2: How can I navigate the iOS interface on my iPhone 14 Pro Max?

Navigating iOS on the iPhone 14 Pro Max is intuitive. Swipe up from the bottom to access the Control Center for quick settings. Swipe down from the top right for notifications. To go back to the home screen, swipe up from the bottom or press the home button. Use gestures like pinch-to-zoom and swipe to switch between apps.

Q 3: What are some common touch gestures I should master on my iPhone 14 Pro Max?

Key touch gestures include tapping to open apps, double-tapping to zoom in on webpages or photos, and using two fingers to scroll. To access the app switcher, swipe up from the bottom and pause. Swipe left or right to switch between apps. These gestures make navigation a breeze.

Q 4: How do I manage apps and notifications effectively on my iPhone 14 Pro Max?

You can organize your apps into folders for easier access. To manage notifications, go to "Settings" > "Notifications." Here, you can customize which apps can send you notifications and how they appear on your screen, helping you stay in control of your device.

Q 5: How can I make calls and send messages using my iPhone 14 Pro Max?

Making calls is as simple as tapping the "Phone" app and selecting a contact. To send messages, open the "Messages" app, tap the compose button, and choose a recipient. You can send texts, photos, videos, and even voice messages with ease.

Q 6: What are the steps to use FaceTime and video calls on my iPhone 14 Pro Max?

FaceTime is a video-calling feature. Open the "FaceTime" app, select a contact, and tap the video camera icon to start a video call. You can also make video calls using other apps like WhatsApp or Skype by selecting a contact and choosing the video call option.

Q 7: How do I set up and manage my email, contacts, and social media accounts on the iPhone 14 Pro Max?

To set up email, go to "Settings" > "Mail" > "Accounts" and select your email provider. Contacts can be managed through the "Contacts" app, where you can add, edit, or delete contacts. For social media, download the respective apps from the App Store and log in with your account credentials.

Q 8: How can I enjoy music, videos, and podcasts on my iPhone 14 Pro Max?

You can use the pre-installed "Music" and "Podcasts" apps for music and podcasts. For videos, the "TV" app is your go-to. You can also explore the App Store for additional media apps like Spotify, YouTube, and Netflix.

Q 9: How do I access news and information on my iPhone 14 Pro Max?

The "News" app provides access to a wide range of news sources. You can also use Safari to browse the web for news websites. Additionally, consider downloading news apps from the App Store for tailored content.

Q 10: How can I explore the App Store for apps and games?

Open the "App Store" app and browse or search for apps and games. You can read reviews, view screenshots, and tap "Get" to download them. Remember to check for updates regularly in the "Updates" tab.

Q 11: What are some tips for taking and editing photos on my iPhone 14 Pro Max?

To take photos, open the "Camera" app and tap the shutter button. Use the editing tools in the "Photos" app to enhance your pictures. You can crop, adjust brightness, and apply filters to make your photos even better.

Q 12: How do I record and share videos with my iPhone 14 Pro Max?

To record videos, open the "Camera" app, and swipe to the "Video" mode. Tap the red record button to start and stop recording. You can share videos by selecting the video in your Photos app and tapping the share button.

Q 13: How can I organize my media library, including photos and videos?

The "Photos" app allows you to create albums and organize your media. You can also use the "Files" app to manage files and folders on your device. Consider using cloud services like iCloud for automatic backup and organization.

Q 14: What's the process for managing preferences and settings on my iPhone 14 Pro Max?

You can access settings by tapping "Settings" on your home screen. Here, you can customize various aspects of your device, including display brightness, sound, notifications, privacy settings, and more. Explore these options to tailor your iPhone to your preferences.

Q 15: Are there accessibility features on the iPhone 14 Pro Max for seniors?

Absolutely. The iPhone offers a range of accessibility features to make it user-friendly for seniors. You can adjust text size, enable voice commands, and activate features like VoiceOver for spoken feedback. Explore the "Accessibility" settings to find options that suit your needs.

Q 16: What should I do if I encounter common issues with my iPhone 14 Pro Max?

Common issues like app crashes or connectivity problems can be resolved by restarting your device, updating apps, or checking for software updates. If you're still facing issues, consider reaching out to Apple Support or consulting online forums for solutions.

PRO SETTINGS FOR YOUR PHOTOS

In the ever-evolving world of smartphone technology, the iPhone has consistently set the bar high for photography. The iPhone 14 Pro Max, with its advanced camera capabilities, takes mobile photography to new heights. For seniors who want to make the most of their iPhone 14 Pro Max camera, understanding and utilizing the pro settings can significantly enhance their photography experience. This chapter is a guide to help seniors navigate the intricate world of pro settings for capturing stunning photos with their iPhone 14 Pro Max.

Understanding the iPhone 14 Pro Max Camera System

Before delving into the pro settings, it's crucial to grasp the fundamentals of the iPhone 14 Pro Max camera system. The iPhone 14 Pro Max boasts a triple-lens camera system, consisting of a wide-angle lens, an ultra-wide-angle lens, and a telephoto lens. These lenses offer various perspectives and focal lengths, allowing seniors to capture a wide range of scenes, from expansive landscapes to detailed close-ups.

Additionally, the iPhone 14 Pro Max is equipped with advanced imaging technologies, such as Deep Fusion and Smart HDR 3, which optimize image quality and enhance details in both bright and low-light environments. Understanding the interplay of these components lays the foundation for mastering the pro settings.

Accessing Pro Settings on iPhone 14 Pro Max

To access the pro settings on the iPhone 14 Pro Max, seniors need to launch the Camera app and select the "Pro" mode. This mode provides manual control over critical camera settings, allowing users to tailor their photos to their preferences and the specific conditions they are shooting in.

The pro settings include:

- **Shutter Speed**: Controls the duration for which the camera's sensor is exposed to light. A faster shutter speed freezes motion, while a slower speed allows for more light and motion blur.
- **ISO Sensitivity**: Adjusts the camera's sensitivity to light. Higher ISO values are useful in low-light conditions but may introduce more noise or graininess in the image.
- **White Balance**: Determines the color temperature of the photo. Seniors can choose from preset options like daylight, cloudy, tungsten, etc., or manually adjust to achieve the desired color tones.
- **Focus**: Enables seniors to manually focus on a specific subject, especially helpful for achieving a sharp focus on a subject against a busy background.
- **Exposure Compensation**: Controls the overall brightness of the image. Seniors can increase or decrease the exposure to achieve the desired lighting for their photos.

Optimizing Shutter Speed for Different Scenarios

Understanding how to optimize shutter speed is fundamental to capturing sharp and well-exposed photos. Seniors can tailor the shutter speed based on the specific scenario they are photographing:

- **Fast Shutter Speed (1/500 sec and above)**: Ideal for capturing fast-moving subjects, such as sports events or birds in flight, without motion blur.
- **Moderate Shutter Speed (1/125 - 1/500 sec)**: Suitable for general photography, ensuring sharpness while allowing for some motion blur in the background or foreground.
- **Slow Shutter Speed (1/30 sec and below)**: Useful for low-light conditions or artistic effects, like light trails or smooth water flow in landscapes.

Mastering ISO Sensitivity for Varied Lighting Conditions

ISO sensitivity determines how the camera sensor responds to light. Seniors can adapt the ISO setting to the lighting conditions they are photographing in:

- **Low ISO (e.g., ISO 100)**: Ideal for bright, well-lit environments. It minimizes noise and maintains image quality.
- **Moderate ISO (e.g., ISO 400 - 800)**: Suitable for typical indoor or moderately lit scenes. It balances image quality and noise.
- **High ISO (e.g., ISO 1600 and above)**: Best for low-light situations, as it enhances sensitivity to light. However, it may introduce some graininess or noise.

Understanding White Balance for Accurate Color Representation

White balance ensures that the colors in a photograph appear natural and true to life. Seniors can adjust the white balance setting to match the lighting conditions:

- **Daylight**: Suitable for outdoor, sunny conditions to maintain accurate color tones.
- **Cloudy**: Ideal for overcast or cloudy days, adding warmth to the image.
- **Tungsten**: Appropriate for indoor lighting or scenes dominated by artificial tungsten lighting, balancing the color temperature.
- **Custom White Balance**: Seniors can manually adjust the color temperature to match the ambient lighting accurately.

Enhancing Focus for Sharp, Clear Images

The focus setting is crucial for achieving sharpness in photographs. Seniors can utilize the manual focus feature to bring their intended subject into sharp focus:

- **Tap to Focus**: Simply tap on the screen to focus on a particular area or subject. The camera will adjust the focus and exposure accordingly.
- **Manual Focus**: Slide the focus bar left or right to manually adjust the focus point, ensuring sharpness on the desired subject.

Balancing Exposure with Exposure Compensation

Exposure compensation allows seniors to control the overall brightness of their photos. It's particularly useful when the automatic exposure setting doesn't achieve the desired lighting:

- **Increasing Exposure (+)**: Brightens the image, helpful when the photo appears underexposed or too dark.
- **Decreasing Exposure (-)**: Darkens the image, useful for correcting overexposed or overly bright photos.

Practical Tips for Using Pro Settings

Mastering pro settings takes practice and experimentation. Here are some practical tips to help seniors make the most of the iPhone 14 Pro Max pro settings:

- **Practice Regularly**: Experiment with different settings and scenarios to understand how each setting affects the final image.
- **Use a Tripod**: For slower shutter speeds, especially in low-light conditions, using a tripod can significantly improve image sharpness.
- **Take Test Shots**: Capture a few test shots with different settings to evaluate which combination works best for a particular scene.

- **Study Results**: Review the images captured with various settings to understand the impact on image quality, sharpness, and color.

Understanding and utilizing the pro settings on the iPhone 14 Pro Max can empower seniors to elevate their photography skills and capture remarkable photos. By mastering shutter speed, ISO sensitivity, white balance, focus, and exposure compensation, seniors can tailor their images to suit different lighting conditions and subjects. With practice and experimentation, seniors can unlock the full potential of their iPhone 14 Pro Max camera, capturing memories with precision and artistry.

CONCLUSION

As we reach the final pages of this simplified iPhone guide for seniors, it is my sincere hope that you are now fully prepared and excited to start using your iPhone 14 Pro Max to its fullest potential. We have covered a comprehensive range of topics, from the absolute basics of navigating iOS to leveraging the phone's many features for communication, entertainment, practical use, and enhanced wellbeing.

If some of the initial terminology and touch gestures felt foreign at first, take heart in knowing that with consistent practice over time, it all becomes second nature. Don't be discouraged if you need to refer back to earlier sections for a refresher. Mastering any new skill requires repetition, and using an iPhone is no different. The most important thing is maintaining a positive attitude and a willingness to learn.

By now, you should have a foundational knowledge of your iPhone's core applications for tasks like making calls, messaging loved ones, taking photos, accessing apps, browsing the internet, and more. We have simplified and demystified the technology in an encouraging, accessible way for non-tech-savvy seniors. With continued use, you will become increasingly proficient at operating your device independently.

Remember, there is no shame in asking for help from younger family members or the Apple support team. Using your iPhone should be an empowering and enjoyable experience. So do not hesitate to have someone walk through a function with you again if needed. With each small breakthrough, you build greater confidence in your abilities.

I hope this guide has succeeded in its mission of making iPhone usage not only manageable but delightful for you. These incredible devices truly offer seniors like yourself tremendous opportunities to stay engaged, informed, connected, and independent. By learning to fully utilize your iPhone 14 Pro Max, you open doors to enhance your life in so many ways:

- Remain active and social by calling, texting, video chatting with loved ones
- Receive important news, weather, and emergency alerts instantly
- Access endless entertainment like music, shows, movies, and books
- Capture special memories and moments with the camera
- Use maps and GPS for simplified navigation and travel
- Enjoy apps, games, online shopping, and more with a tap
- Monitor health, finances, schedules, and everyday tasks

- Express creativity through photos, videos, writing, and sharing
- Discover resources to pursue hobbies and passions
- Feel safe with emergency SOS features if help is needed

My greatest wish is that by reading this guide, you feel empowered to embrace these possibilities and truly get the most from your technology. With simplified knowledge and the right approach, you absolutely can master your iPhone 14 Pro Max.

Remember to celebrate every small win. Stay patient, creative and curious. Seek help when needed. Approach it with a learning mindset. If you follow this process, you will be amazed at just how intuitive using an iPhone can become. Soon you will wonder how you ever lived without it!

I am rooting for your success. Never stop pursuing knowledge and self-betterment. You are never too old to learn new skills. I hope this book has instilled confidence to continue expanding your digital capabilities. The future belongs to those who approach it with an open and willing mindset.

You now hold the knowledge. You have the power. Go embrace the incredible, limitless potential of technology to improve and enrich your life. Your iPhone adventure awaits.

INDEX

Made in the USA
Middletown, DE
02 March 2024

- Express creativity through photos, videos, writing, and sharing
- Discover resources to pursue hobbies and passions
- Feel safe with emergency SOS features if help is needed

My greatest wish is that by reading this guide, you feel empowered to embrace these possibilities and truly get the most from your technology. With simplified knowledge and the right approach, you absolutely can master your iPhone 14 Pro Max.

Remember to celebrate every small win. Stay patient, creative and curious. Seek help when needed. Approach it with a learning mindset. If you follow this process, you will be amazed at just how intuitive using an iPhone can become. Soon you will wonder how you ever lived without it!

I am rooting for your success. Never stop pursuing knowledge and self-betterment. You are never too old to learn new skills. I hope this book has instilled confidence to continue expanding your digital capabilities. The future belongs to those who approach it with an open and willing mindset.

You now hold the knowledge. You have the power. Go embrace the incredible, limitless potential of technology to improve and enrich your life. Your iPhone adventure awaits.

INDEX

Made in the USA
Middletown, DE
02 March 2024

50684893R00044